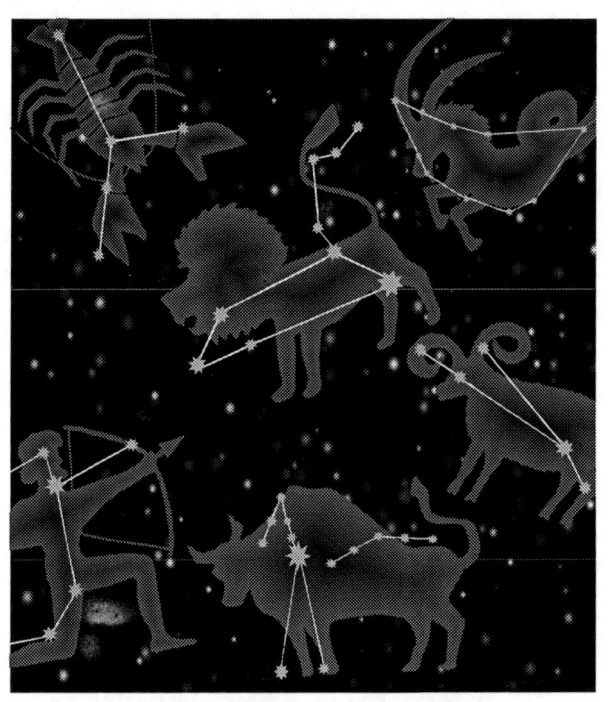

ZODIAC

BEDFORDSHIRE

Edited by Donna Samworth

First published in Great Britain in 2002 by
YOUNG WRITERS
Remus House,
Coltsfoot Drive,
Peterborough, PE2 9JX
Telephone (01733) 890066

All Rights Reserved

Copyright Contributors 2002

HB ISBN 0 75433 524 0
SB ISBN 0 75433 525 9

FOREWORD

Young Writers was established in 1991 with the aim of promoting creative writing in children, to make reading and writing poetry fun.

Once again, this year proved to be a tremendous success with over 41,000 entries received nationwide.

The Zodiac competition has shown us the high standard of work and effort that children are capable of today. The competition has given us a vivid insight into the thoughts and experiences of today's younger generation. It is a reflection of the enthusiasm and creativity that teachers have injected into their pupils, and it shines clearly within this anthology.

The task of selecting poems was a difficult one, but nevertheless, an enjoyable experience. We hope you are as pleased with the final selection in *Zodiac Bedfordshire* as we are.

CONTENTS

Bedford High School

Frances Bennett	1
Danielle Hinckley	2
Eleanor Reeds	2
Mary Wood	3

Icknield High School

Hajrah Javed	3
Ryan Bain	4
Samuel Hull	4
David Greaves	5
Rachael Bamgboye	5
Thomas Freeman	6
Shyam Patel	7
Alex Whitlock	8
Sadia Shabir	8
Fabian Satchwell	9
Laura Jayne Garner	10
Kaylee Ludlow	10
Gemma Magill	11
Zara Iqbal	11
Katie B Keene	12
Shireen Simms	12
Niraj Shah	13
Sheetal Bharadia	13
Daniel Atkinson	14
Amy Howells	14
Thomas Mills	15
Donna Fletcher	16
Simone Emmanuel	16
Robbie Roe	17
Andrew Thomas	18
Jenna Hewitt	18
Matthew Maitland	19
Tanita Satchwell	20

David Tither	20
Kayleigh Abrus	21
Charlotte Messer	21
Lucy Butler	22
John Wyatt	22
Chris Stone	23
Heather Sygrove	24
Caroline Wallbank	24
Laura Venant	25
Atif Hussain	25
Samantha Francis	26
Stephen Herrity	26
Timothy Wildridge	27
Louise Shearn	27
Lois McCulley	28
Sophia Tirelli	28
Sarah Brennan	29
Gemma Rutherford	30
Bhavash Karsan	30
Kamal Barrie	31
Philip Risby	31
Chris O'Neil	32
Emma Lambert	32
Josh Aarons	33
Scott Courtney	34
Adil Farooq	34
Sarah Heatherwick	35
Edward McDermott	35
Victoria Heywood	36
Ebrahim Parkar	36
Rebecca Findlay	37
Michael Pearson	37
Luke Edgeley	38
Simon Hayes	38
Sabina Haque	39
Jaleela Ahmed	40
Andy Greaves	41
Hitesh Patel	42

Umer Hakeem	42
Lauren Bowyer	43
Robin Cooper	44
Emily Quince	44
Lewi Saunders	45
Gemma Hales	46
Toby Henness	46
Rebecca Ashby	47
Tanya Blacksley	47
Katie Olde	48
Tom Connelly	48
Craig Edwards	49
Amy Rickman	49
Sarah Sackey	50
Alex Crawley	50
Daniel Johnston	51
Kallum Cotcher	51
David Thomas	52
Caroline Lawson	52
Rebecca Witterick	53
Rebecca Hendy	54
Jade Newns	54
Holly French	55
Lisa Curran	56
Lauren Watson	56
Charlotte Perrott	57
Elizabeth Burch	57
Pawandip Bahia	58
Tom Rollins	58
Lukhneet Bajwa	59
Kurt Lambert	59
Rachel Underwood	60
Paul McSkimming	60
Amy Venant	61
Jade Thomas	62
Charlotte Norman	62
Matthew Gascoine	63
Sam Sherwood	64

Alannah Brennan	64
Lauren Dinham	65
Naweed Darr	65
Nazish Mehreen	66
Chris Michell	66
Joanne Webb	67
Loren Hennessy Leach	67
Jessica Charles	68
Jessica Fisher	68
Thomas Kelby	69
Elliott Fensome	69
Sarah White	70
Kathryn Rouse	71
Menal Katechia	72
Laura Yaxley	72
Saminah Begum	73
Chris Cordwell	73
Imran Ahmed	74
Chris Kingshott	74
Adam Dodds	75
Matthew Harvey	75
Stacey Marum	76
Laura Golding	76
Ross Colbert	77
Mark Morris	77
Hannah Gormley	78
Sally-Anne Wright	78
Lauren Randall	79
Michael Turner	79
Cassandra Thomas	80
Dipa Tailor	81
Luke Firth	82
Amer Javed	83
Michaela Reid-Thomas	84
Jai Tailor	84
Manjit Sobti	85
Dominic Carrick	85
Natalie McPhee	86

Yasmin Rose	86
Phillippa Gray	87
Rebecca Mathurin	87
Gurpreet Chattha	88
Michaela Blake	88
Amey White	89
Callum Symonds	90
Katie Yau	90
Amy Haggett	91
Sam Gower	92
Carl Jolley	92
Nicola Peet	93
Raymond Poon	93
Dominic Williams	94
Joanne Arnold	94
Hasan Abu	95
Christopher Growestock	95
Kylie-Marie Clarke	96
David Millard	96
Waseem Ayub	97
Emma Aylott	97
Nathaniel Quigley	98
Michael Pridmore	98
Martin Wood	99
Katerina Drimussis	99
James Falconer	100
Casie Eldridge	100
Rachael Anderson	101

Lealands High School

Victoria Wilson	101
Nicola Theodore	102
Paul Barnard	102
Kylie Large	103
Danielle Rosson	104
Chris Clarke	104

Christopher Gallagher	105
Karen Kontoh	106
Jade Goodman	106
Marlon Johnson	107
Amy Fordham	107
Katherine Hannah Woollard	108

Leighton Middle School

Jasmine Pughe	109
Jessica Clough	110
Elizabeth Daniels	111
Maudie Wyatt	112
Lucy Williamson	113
Flora MacPhail	114
Dawn Mayne	114
Lauren Stone	115
Camilla Barbosa-Jefferson	116

Linslade Middle School

Thomas Wood	116
Kevin Edwards	117
Elise Thomas	117
Jo Bailey-Watson	118
Sophie Hing	118
Richard Savill	119
Helen Humphreys	120
Natashia McKenzie-Cook	120
Lisa Baczynski	121
Kerry Mittins	122
Ben East	122
Hayleigh McDonald	123
Philip Trott	123
Samantha Cundell	124
Kieran Billington	125
Christopher George	126
Emma Harfield	126

Laura Keable	127
Laura Taylor	127
Anna Head	128
Caylin Joski-Jethi	129
James Bishop	129
Helen Yates	130
Andrew Reeves	130
Avril Dowdeswell	131
Emily Sheppard	131
Laura Driscoll	132

Luton Sixth Form College

Steven Parker	133
Claire Gazeley	134

Marston Vale Middle School

Lee Turner	134
Miles Sloan	135
Lauren Smith	135
Will Mason-Wilkes	136
Tessa-Louise Tringham	136
Fern Blevins	137
Louise Moynham	137
Christopher Woodward	138
Heather Welsh	138
Daniel Spiers	139
Nicola Coop	140
Natasha Freeman	141
Debbie Fisher	142
Karissa France	142
Richard Collins	143
Hannah Bennett-Cook	143
Tristan Moore	144
David Pugh	145
Ben Eagles	146
Lydia Freeman	146
Kerri Shorter	147

	Victoria Taylor	148
	Mica Smith	148
	Samantha Grummitt	149
	Kayleigh Pratt	149
	Eleanor Jay	150
	Laura Jeffery	150
	Jade Goff	151
	Lucy Hourihan	152
	Melanie Dunne	152
	Amy Mould	153
	Emily-Jane Wilson	153

Mill Vale Middle School

	Abigail Horton	154
	Thomas Peirce	154
	Joanna Solley	155
	Michaela Penny	155
	Danielle McGrath	156
	Adam Regan	156
	Laura Collins	157
	Ian Sharp	157
	Bethany Hilton	158
	Lauren May Mackenzie	158
	Charlotte Smith	159
	Claire Parker	159
	Stuart Lee Nash	160
	David Isaac	160
	Martyn Tallon	161
	Leanne Frimley	161
	Lewis Collins	162
	Elizabeth Sansom	162
	Elliott Jaggs	162
	Rosie Kirby	163

Northfields Upper School

	Aisha Brown	163
	Lucy Partridge	164
	Brenden Delaney	164

Jerome Bellot	165
Megan Scrivener	166
Rachel Scheidegger	166
Sarah Steffens	167
Nicola Botcher	168
Steven Baker	168
Stuart Jones	169
Lian Wollington	169
Victoria Dale	170
Tom King	171
Lisa Holland	172
Peter Byrne	172
Karl Nielsen	173
Michael Smith	173
Kirsty Denning	174
Katy-Anne Jennings	174
Chris Taylor	175
Chris Butcher	175
Nicola Brady	176
Victoria Winchester	177
Sean Barton	178
Sean Bishop	178
Channan Harkin	179
Carl Denning	179
Emma Ford	180
Rachel Chambers	180
Callum Hayden	181
Shameem Hassan	182
Lisa Thomas	182
Paul Henman	183
Elaine Lunt	184
Mark Moore	185
Kayleigh Smithson	186
Luke Gaffer	186
Jenny Hopla	187
Liam Breckon	187

Katherine Mullender	188
Gary Lawrence	188
Emily Wilkinson	189
Jennifer Webb	189
Sarah Hadland	190
Natasha Miles	191
Ashley Jenkinson	192
Kerry Lambert	192
Emily Waller	193
Michelle McGann	193
Nicholas Bunce	194
Daniel Ellis	194
Caroline Impey	195
Matthew Burton	195
Levi Murray	196
Sam Taylorson	196
Christine Baker	197
Lauren E Burrows	198
Sophie Boddington	198
Princy Gor	199
Lydia Conlon	199
Shelley Whitehead	200
Sarah Bithrey	201
Sam Girvan	202
Katie Huggins	202
Ryan Sheahan	203
Fiona Broni	204
Amy Sewell	205
Leana King	206
Charlotte Davis	207
Gary Hudston	208
Kim Loczy	208
Samantha Candler	209
Georgie Atkins	209
Jade Simper	210

Stratton Upper School

Jack Janes	210
Vicky Staines	211
Colin McLeod	211
Megan Williams	212
Dean Kahl	212
Sarah Buckland & Rachel Bennett	213
James Worboys	214
Josh Crisp-Hihn	214
Francesca Wells	215
Michaela Talman	216
Cheryl Barfoot	216
Zoe Atkins	217
Anna Woodall	217
Alice Nuth	218
Holly Johannesen	218
Dominique Braybrooks	219
Kelly Chapman	219
Julie Groves	220
Tracey Spavins	220
Louise Baker	221
Shaun Allen	222
Samuel Jenkins	222
Scott Gore	223
Becky Sutton	223
Natasha Jones	224
Michael Gostling	224
Kayleigh Clement	225
Gemma Potter	226
Jenny Austin	226
Dan Jackson	227
Karen Patman	228
Vicky Pearson	228
Natalie Giddings	229
Claire Rowley	230
Laura Stackhouse	230

David Buss	231
Amie Jeeves	232
Richard Hill	232
Rebecca Setchell	233

Vandyke Upper School
Katherine Bosworth	233
Victoria Miljevic	234

The Poems

JOURNEY THROUGH THE AIR

I'm in the air,
I'm in the sky,
I'm way up high,
1,000 feet and rising fast,
You can see the wind rushing past.

We're over land,
We're over sea,
We're in the clouds and I can't see,
The clouds are white and fluffy too,
Now they're plenty but now they're few.

I'm over fields,
I'm over grass,
I'm over a bypass,
The fields are an emerald patchwork,
And the cars are going to work.

I'm in the air,
I'm slowing down,
I'm going down,
'No, no,' I cry, I start to frown,
But we did, we had to go down.

I'm on the ground,
I'm off the plane,
I'm on dry land again,
I didn't want to end my journey there,
My journey through the air.

Frances Bennett (11)
Bedford High School

MR AND MRS BUBBLEFELT

Mr Bubblefelt had a great life,
he owed it all to his fat little wife.
She'd cook and clean for him,
and answer to his every whim.
One day Mrs Bubblefelt had had enough,
so she decided to get tough.
No longer would she be there,
she was going shopping for something to wear.
Mrs Bubblefelt announced classes in pottery,
the next we'd heard she'd won the lottery.
The postcard said Mrs Bubblefelt was soaking up the sun,
playing beachball in the Carribeann.

Danielle Hinckley (12)
Bedford High School

GRIM REALITY

As I trudge along the street, dragging my feet;
I gaze up at grey heavens, shadows of the night,
The moon is barely visible, 'neath the misty skies.
I glance down to the shallow pools of black,
The pavement is indistinguishable from the grit of the road.
The winter's eve is cold and dreary,
Our fantasy of summer is betrayed,
There is no comfort here nor anywhere.
Christmas contentment is far ahead in our bright future,
No fairy lamps light the way ahead,
For November nights are grim
reality.

Eleanor Reeds (12)
Bedford High School

DELAYS

We thought we'd made a journey,
Of knowledge.
We thought we'd learnt,
After World War II.
The suffering, all for nothing,
All for one man's crazy dreams.
We thought, 'Never
Never again
Will we have that horror,
That horrible catastrophe.'
'See!' we said
'We've made a journey,
Of knowledge
We know what's right now!'
But have we really?
This suffering is still in the world.
Think of America - 11th September.
We're still on square one
After millions of years
Of 'intelligent' life.
We should have made a journey,
But have we yet?

Mary Wood (12)
Bedford High School

THE SNAKE

The green smooth skin,
Slithering through the grass,
Its tongue so red and pointing,
Its eyes shiny as glass,
It moves like a skipping rope through the grass.

Hajrah Javed (12)
Icknield High School

A Starry Night

As I look upon the stars
On the starriest night,
One star stands out
It shines so bright,
I think and think about what it would be like
To be that star on the starriest night.

I had a dream
About that star,
It moves away
It goes so far,
As it goes I ask myself,
Are we friends?
I sure hope we are.

Ryan Bain (12)
Icknield High School

Leo

The mighty king of the jungle
Tough, but loving
A faithful friend,
That encourages dreams,
Kind and helping,
Peridot and Ruby are the jewels
Close to its heart,
He is mighty, fierce and upfront
But can be gentle and generous to others,
Leo is the King!
The everlasting sun!

Samuel Hull (11)
Icknield High School

Zodiac

A galactic world of stars and planets
A vast universe waiting to be explored
Torrents of darkness among the unknown
Deserted and peaceful, but never alone
Adventurous comets that energetically speed by
Unique constellations that lie in our sky
Ghostly galleons that sail by at night
Like bats out of Hell are gone by the morning light
The twelve signs of the Zodiac spread across the magical skies
A belt of heavens along the ecliptic
A vast universe waiting to be explored.

David Greaves (12)
Icknield High School

A Lonely Little Star

I see a star in the sky
A lonely little star it is
Even though it's on its own
It's shining bright like a glow-worm in the night
It leads me where
I do not know
Should I stay
Or should I go
Or should I wait for another day?

Rachael Bamgboye (12)
Icknield High School

ZODIAC (THORPE PARK)

A few miles away,
There is a place,
Which in the end,
Will put a smile on your face.

Open the gates,
Open your eyes,
Say this is great,
What a surprise.

All the rides,
Are too good to be true.
Rollercoasters too,
You're lucky it's you.

Flying Fishes,
And Tidal Wave.
In the memory of your brain,
This is something you'll save.

The bestest ride,
In this place,
Is called Detonator,
Do you want to race?

Some other fun rides,
Like No Escape,
Go fast round corners,
Shattering like space.

There's an American ride,
In 2002,
It's got ten loops,
For people like you.

I've got to go now,
I've had a good time,
I'll visit again,
Some other time.

Thomas Freeman (12)
Icknield High School

ZODIAC

When I think of Zodiac
I think of the stars
If only, there was life on Mars.

When I think of Zodiac
I think of the moon
It looks just like the cheese that I eat with a spoon.

When I think of Zodiac
I think of rockets
They look like the ones on my trouser pockets.

When I think of Zodiac
I think of the night
Even the word Zodiac gives me a fright.

When I think of Zodiac
I think of the Milky Way
Just like the chocolate, I eat every day.

When I think of Zodiac
I think of star signs
Everybody knows that Cancer is mine.

Shyam Patel (12)
Icknield High School

A Long Lost Alien

If you go up to space
You'll find a wicked place
There are stars in the sky
Sitting beside a long lost planet

On that long lost planet
There is a long lost city
In that long lost city lived an alien
When this long lost alien was sad he'd look up

He would look up at the long lost stars
The long lost stars would be shining bright
If he looked to his left he would see long lost alien kids having fun
If he looked to his right he would see long lost nothing

On that long lost nothing he built a long lost house
He lived in the long lost house until . . .
One day a long lost comet crashed his long lost house to a long lost pea
So he went back to the long lost city and lived happily ever after

But then the long lost . . . I don't think so!

Alex Whitlock (12)
Icknield High School

Autumn Fires

In the other garden and all up the vale
From the autumn bonfire see the smoke trailing
Pleasant summer is over
All the flowers have lost their colour
The red fire of autumn
Fire blazing and grey smoke
Towering in the air

Sing a song of the seasons
Something to brighten it all up
Flowers in the summer
Fires in the fall
And stars twinkling in the sky at night
And the moon is shining brighter than ever.

Sadia Shabir (12)
Icknield High School

FAIRGROUND SPOOKS

I was enjoying myself in a fairground
I passed the fortune teller's hut
Where I heard a mysterious sound
I'm going, I've got guts

She said,
'I know who you are
You're Simon Patella
Scorpio's your star
And you've been a bad little fella.

You'll find yourself in life-threatening trouble
A man will chase, wanting to take your life
You're going to have to run on the double
Be careful the man has a knife.'

I went out the hut
What did I see?
I saw an angry man
Looking at me.

Fabian Satchwell (11)
Icknield High School

YOGA

I'm sitting here, my legs are crossed,
My instructor's chanting, 'Ummm.'
Am I supposed to be finding inner peace
Because I'm just sitting on my bum.

I look at the people around me,
Gee, they look so weird,
I just realised this isn't a women's class,
Someone has a beard.

I close my eyes,
It all goes dark,
I start to chant,
It's like the humming of a lark.
The lesson's over now,
Just when I was getting the hang of this Yoga thing,
I am amazed at my self, oh wow!

Laura Jayne Gardner (11)
Icknield High School

A TWINKLING STAR!

A little star twinkles bright
In the darkness of the night
In the blue mysterious sky
The twinkling star is very shy
The twinkling star flashes twice
Doesn't this sight look so nice
The twinkling star is joined by another
The two bright stars twinkle at each other
Soon the twinkling star goes away
'Oh please little star, come back another day.'

Kaylee Ludlow (13)
Icknield High School

QUESTIONS?

Twelve months of a year.
How many horoscopes have been read?
What shapes will the stars be in tonight?
Has Mars forgotten its toffee centre?
Has the Milky Way lost is creamy centre?
Questions. Questions!
All of which need some answers.
And does the Galaxy still melt in your mouth?
Is the Black Hole full of magic?
Does the Black Hole have a secret centre?
Questions. Questions!
All of which need some answers.

Gemma Magill (12)
Icknield High School

STAR SIGNS

S   tar signs are for different months
T   oday I wonder what they will predict for me
A   wonderful day ahead or a miserable day
R   member it's only a star sign.

S   o just don't live your life by them
I   see the stars at night shine so bright
G   reat is that meteor ball that flew past
N   ovember is the month I wait for
S   ights so wonderful over the North Pole.

Zara Iqbal (11)
Icknield High School

MY STAR SIGN

October was the month that I was born,
Because I'm balanced I'm never torn,
Libra is my star sign,
Opal the stone too, is mine,
Because I'm a snake I'm a slippery creature,
But loyalty is my main redeeming feature,
I can always talk my way out of trouble,
Gemini's are my friends, they are double.

Leo and Pisces are on my side,
But because I'm fair, the rules I abide,
I can see both sides of a quarrel,
First impressions count is my moral,
Art, music and drama, that's for me,
Because I'm a Libra, peacemaking is my key.

Katie B Keene (12)
Icknield High School

CAPRICORN!

C unning and courageous
A nnoying and aerodynamic
P layful but personal
R adical and really fast
I nsane but interesting
C orny and childish
O h so nice and obedient
R eady for anything and restless
N asty (sometimes) but nice.

Shireen Simms (11)
Icknield High School

STARZ!

Up in the misty sky,
The little stars there they lie.
From morning to night,
The tiny stars shine their light.
From galaxy to galaxy,
There they will be,
Over there you see.
From shooting, flying, nova stars,
Some have even come past Mars.
One day will they finally go?
What do you think?
I say no!

Niraj Shah (12)
Icknield High School

THE NIGHT SKY

The sun has gone down
and out comes the mysterious night sky.
The moon looks misty
but glistens as the wolves howl.
The stars have a gold and silver colour in them,
which shines through the night.
You can see horoscopes.
Aries, Pisces or Leo.
The dark sky is unknown to many people
because it is mysterious and creepy.

Sheetal Bharadia (11)
Icknield High School

COMPUTERS

Computers, computers: what wondrous machines
You can add, subtract, divide and even multiply
On such simple programs such as Excel,
And there's even a calculator!
I can type homework in Word,
Make birthday cards in Publisher,
Make a slide show in Powerpoint,
And send faxes in Access.
I can learn German in a click of a finger,
Find information on Encarta,
Use knowledge in Countdown,
Research facts and figures on the Internet,
And receive E-mails in Outlook Express.
I can print on my Lexmark printer,
And scan on my Mustek scanner.
I can save my work onto my hard drive,
And I often make a backup onto a floppy.
I can play games, that I buy,
And I have a lot of fun!
With a computer the possibilities are endless,
Where would the world be without them?

Daniel Atkinson (12)
Icknield High School

ZODIAC IS...

Zodiac is star signs, based around the time of birth
Zodiac is the months, a personal place on Earth
Zodiac is elements, water, earth, fire, air
Zodiac is horoscopes, never seeming very fair.

Zodiac is constellations, a grouping of stars
Zodiac is planets, Venus, Earth and Mars
Zodiac is the sun and moon giving out light
Zodiac is space, darker than the darkest night.

Amy Howells (12)
Icknield High School

LIFE IN THE ARMY!

Up at the crack of dawn,
Get out of bed and take a long yawn,
Hear the sergeant's big boot stomps coming past,
Make sure you get dressed and line up *fast!*
Watch the door slowly creak open and watch the sergeant walk past,
Is this the first time or is this the last?
Time to get out and start the day,
Don't fool around, this is work not play,
Through mud and grass the rain comes down fast!
Your clothes are a state but look at your mate,
He's just as muddy so you don't have to worry
Just feel great.
The sergeant comes out to congratulate you,
He gives you a medal, he must approve of your excellence and skill,
You are spoken to as everyone else stands still.
Feeling happy you and the gang go back to the hut,
Get washed and changed, get rid of the muck,
Eat your cooked roast steak till you're full up.
Then go to bed and get ready to get up for another day of Life
In the *army*.

Thomas Mills (12)
Icknield High School

IF I COULD FLY

Stars, planets and other stuff make up the sky
Sometimes I wish I could fly
Just to touch them
I would meet there mysterious aliens and greet them
We would have a friendly chat

I would then fly past the planets onto the stars
And from there I can see Mars
Their bright shine twinkling on me
I would relax and see the moon
See you there

I sit on the moon wondering as it gets darker
I will explore the crater and find out new things
Better fly back
Why don't you come with me?

Into my bed I will fall
Acting like nothing happened at all
My mum would come and check on me
But I would be fast asleep, when she goes I will wake
And then wonder again about the world I live in.

Donna Fletcher (11)
Icknield High School

THE UNIVERSE

It's strange how far away stars are,
yet they seem so near.
They twinkle, twinkle in the sky,
and are there for the whole year.

The moon so high in the sky,
gives us light through the night.
The sun shining on its side,
makes it look so bright.

The planets floating round us,
giving us land to explore.
Venus, Mars and Jupiter,
as well as many more.

The universe is our home,
we're all here together,
and hopefully we'll be here,
for ever and ever and ever.

Simone Emmanuel (11)
Icknield High School

ZODIAC POEM

The small sailing boat rocking in the Mediterranean Sea
carrying no one but two souls.
The sea calm with barely a wave in the next mile.
But come nightfall it was rough and strong.
The powerful cold deep ocean had saved up its strength
for the dark starry night.
As the hours went by, the waves were up to a dozen feet.
The small stubby man swung the weak wooden door open
letting his much the same looking wife into the cabin to be safe.
As the clock ticked the waves shook the boat around
with sail and steering pole shaking around
sending the light wooden invention sideways and rocking it wildly.
The waves were up to three dozen feet high
soaking the once bone dry rusty wood.
Finally the sun rose when the clock struck six.
The ruins of the ship finally pulled up on shore.
The two innocent souls stumbled out.
Relief!
'We are alive.'

Robbie Roe (12)
Icknield High School

NO ONE

No one has no food,
No one has no water,
No one has no name,
He has, for as far as I see, no future.

But no one has a home,
No one has a life,
No one has a body,
And yes, he has a present, just about.

Though no one had a kingdom,
No one had an audience,
No one had luxury and leisure,
He had a golden past.

> No one's sorrow is unheard,
> His crying is silent,
> His suffering is hidden,
> It was as if he did not exist,
> But he was definitely real,
> Because no one is someone,
> And someone is very special.

Andrew Thomas (12)
Icknield High School

WHAT ARE STARS?

Stars are yellow, stars are bright, stars gleam during the night.
The sky is black, the stars make light making the sky partly bright.

Stars are mysterious, why are they there?
If you look carefully you can see a great bear.

Stars appear at the end of the day,
When they're together they make the Milky Way.

Stars they twinkle whilst you dream,
Things aren't always what they seem.

Nice and frosty, stars shine bright,
Help to light up the darkest night.

Stars can guide you when you're lost,
Stars are planets in our cosmos.

Jenna Hewitt (11)
Icknield High School

THE MAN WHO WENT TO THE MOON

There once was a man, who went to the moon,
But he felt a bit of a prune.

For he was the only person to be seen,
Except for the Martians dressed in green.

As he looked at the stars,
It seemed to make him sad because it reminded him of his ma.

As he looked deeper in,
It seemed to be like a big black bin.

Filled up with bright stars,
And colourful planets.

But as he watched the shooting stars pass by,
And the UFOs flying

He thought to himself,
'Why did I come up here?'

Matthew Maitland (12)
Icknield High School

STAR GAZING

Do you look at the stars?
Ever tried to read them?
What makes them glow, sparkle, shine and glitter?
Holds them there, keeps them there,
Never tries to move them?
Glittering at night, silent in the day.
Where do they go when the sun comes out?
Why don't they sit and stay?
How comes they make a pattern?
What story do they tell?
What is it that makes them come and go?
Cancer and Scorpio,
Capricorn and Aquarius,
Aries and Leo,
Pisces and Sagittarius,
Libra and Virgo,
Gemini and Taurus,
All putting on a show.
Sleeping through the day,
Coming out at night,
Now I must leave to
Watch them glow.

Tanita Satchwell (12)
Icknield High School

WAR

The men are waiting to go to war,
They all look down to the floor with depressed faces,
The tank makes everything rumble,
The dull skies add to the depressed armies,
The men go to war!

David Tither (13)
Icknield High School

STARRY SKY

Strong stars in the sky
Come out at night
They shine out nice and bright.
Wow, they must have a lot of might.
Flashing stars, dull stars
They're all the same.
Sometimes you can even play a game.
Strong stars in the sky
How nice they are.
Especially when they flicker.
There's lots of shapes in the stars.
Why would there be such things as Mars.
I suppose I've got to end this now.

Kayleigh Ambrus (11)
Icknield High School

STARS

Now it's night,
Look up at the stars,
Shining bright,
The winged horse,
Takes flight,
The great bear,
Facing the west,
Is remembered best,
A cluster of stars,
Make the scales
Waiting to weigh the sunlight,
And as dawn approaches,
They fade away.

Charlotte Messer (11)
Icknield High School

STARS

The stars shine brightly in the sky,
As the night passes by,
Big ones and small ones,
They all glisten and glow,
Each one is different,
Do you want to know?
There are twelve altogether,
They are: Capricorn, Cancer and Aquarius,
Gemini, Libra and Sagittarius,
Taurus, Pisces and Virgo,
Scorpio, Aries and . . .?
Oh yeah, Leo, that's me!
They all have their own meanings,
And now you know all the signs,
They have a different quality,
So which one are you?

Lucy Butler (12)
Icknield High School

THE KILLING

A woman screams
The killer steps forward
He brings back his knife
And slits her throat

He wipes the blood off his knife
'You killed her, she was my wife,'
Said a man walking in with a gun in his hand
He shoots the killer down to the ground

With tears in his eyes
He said in his head,
'Now you know what it's like
To be dead.'

John Wyatt (13)
Icknield High School

THE BOMB

The bomb's being dropped
Onto the brown muddy farmland
The soldiers look over the tank's edge
Being told what to do next.

Near misses by the falling bombs
Onto the tyre-tracked farmland
Soldiers climbing over the tank's edge
Being told what to do next.

Slowly the soldiers progress
Getting muddy and dirty
Lying as still as the blade of grass
Being told what to do next.

Bombs falling heavily
Soldiers being killed
Screams and bangs filling the air
Being told what to do next.

A big explosion as the bunker gets hit
The tank's gun is non-stop
Two planes come spiralling down
Hoping to be told to go home next.

Chris Stone (13)
Icknield High School

What Is Fire?

Fire is the flaming eyes of a tiger
Stalking a herd of unsuspecting antelope.

It is the pressure being released in thrashing form of snakes' tails
From the centre of the Earth, shaking and rattling.

It is the wisping tails of devil horses
Flaring in frantic pace.

Fire is the golden hem of a dancer's dress
Twisting and shaking to the erratic beat.

It is the golden petals on a Red Hot Poker
Swaying in the fresh breezy air.

It is the sparks of steel
Clashing on a blacksmith's anvil.

That is fire.

Heather Sygrove (13)
Icknield High School

Space And Beyond

Z odiac is a very strange unknown thing
O ut of this world into the big black thing
D ecorated with lots of stars and planets like Mars
I t is our galaxy and our universe
A nd holds our solar system
C ontaining planets Mercury and Mars.

Caroline Wallbank (11)
Icknield High School

IN THE RAIN

Dark grey clouds hang in the sky,
The streets become empty as the weather sets in.
Ladies hide beneath umbrellas as they race across the street,
Heels click-clicking against cold brick roads.
The thunderstorm grows close.

Look further into the picture,
Look for the man in the black.
Slipping a purse out of a bag too quick for you to see,
Watch out when you see him walking about,
It could be your purse he's after.

Dark grey clouds hang in the sky,
The streets become empty as the weather sets in.
Ladies hide beneath umbrellas as they race across the street,
Heels click-clicking against cold brick roads.
The thunderstorm grows close.

Laura Venant (13)
Icknield High School

THINGS THAT ARE IN SPACE

P   lanets in space
L   ots of meteoroids coming in pace
A   spaceship zooming through
N   o gravity though
E   erie things that happen out there
T   he shooting stars coming out of nowhere
S   ome people looking up in the sky wondering what is up there.

Atif Hussain (11)
Icknield High School

STAR SIGN

My star sign is Aquarius
It is a person in water
My star sign means:
Smile to yourself as you realise
that you've mistakenly taken the comments of a loved one
or close friend in quite the wrong way.
Rather than be upset, you should write it off as silly but important.
The same cannot be said, however, for issues revolving around work,
money or perhaps property,
because you'll hear talk of moves about to be made
and your name will feature in most of the conversations.
This might make one or two other people uneasy
because they'll feel they're being overshadowed by you.
Relish the ease with which you give them the kind of reassurance
they need.

Samantha Francis (12)
Icknield High School

MOTHER SHIP

S olar system is all around us.
O rbiting. We orbit the sun.
L eo, 24th July to the 23rd August.
A ries, 21st March to the 20th April.
R ejected, the people who wanted to go into space.

S atellites help us get in touch with family.
Y ou sitting on Earth.
S omeone in NASA.
T elephone your family.
E merge, the stars emerge at night.
M other ship, taking us where we want to go.

Stephen Herrity (11)
Icknield High School

WHO AM I?

Am I Tim, a simple person?
Am I the sea, deep and unknown?
Am I praised or eternally damned?
Am I God's child or Satan's spawn?
Am I good at things or do I just get lucky?
Am I full of valour or a cowardly dog?
Am I a clear thinker or a delusional fool?
Am I trying too hard or not hard enough?
Am I controlled or free of will?
Am I sheltered or left bare beneath the sun?
Am I a single person or a piece of the big puzzle?
If I am none of those then
Who am I and what is my purpose?

Timothy Wildridge (13)
Icknield High School

THE CHINESE TIGER

Peaceful, pretty
the moon is bright,
a perfect night.
She peeks her head out of the bush.
Her thin chin, her beautiful brow,
she slips her graceful paw out
and lays it on the ground.
She pulls her body out,
her body perfect for its job.
Bright eyes and always alert,
she awaits in the grass for her prey . . .

Louise Shearn (12)
Icknield High School

ZODIAC!

The 12 strange stars with very different names
Each one of them more mysterious than the other;
Capricorn is a mountain goat who has a lot of pride,
Aquarius is the mysterious water carrier,
Aries is the ram who is big, bold and beautiful,
Cancer is the crab who stands strong,
Leo is the lion who is a strong leader with a big, brave heart,
Virgo is the young virgin who is very beautiful and petite,
Libra is the set of scales who sees everything two ways,
Scorpio is the animal who has a nasty sting,
Sagittarius is a half man, half goat who has faith
In everyone and everything,
Pisces is the fish who has a strong fin,
Gemini are the twins who are completely different,
Taurus is the bull who is stronger than an ox.

Lois McCulley (12)
Icknield High School

BLACKOUT

Dark deep layers of twinkling stars,
Planets lie, questions to ask.
Jupiter's eye staring right through,
Fog of Neptune, sea of green and blue.
Mars' rocks and rusted iron.
Dusty pink skylines, looking over craters, beyond craters.

Leo's roar,
Scorpio's sting.
Taurus' horns,
Gemini's twin.

All of this in one big world,
A world of jet black skies and stars.
How and why, I hear you shout,
A world I like to call my Blackout!

Sophia Tirelli (11)
Icknield High School

PRECIOUS RAIN

The sound of the crystal rain splashed onto the street
Forming puddles that sparkle in the sunlight.
Pairs of soaking wet feet splashed onto the cobbled street
Making ripples like waves far out to sea.
As the precious diamond rain continues to fall.

As umbrellas are pushed up people rush for shelter
Different varieties of feelings fill the misty air.
Women become miserable as their feet get wet.
Small children become joyful as they splash playfully in the puddles.
As the precious diamond rain continues to fall.

The strong, forceful wind blows through the diamond rain.
Umbrellas are turned inside out as the gale blows.
People are no now unprotected as their umbrellas fly out of their hands.
The light, misty rain wets everything it touches.
The precious diamond rain continues to fall.

People's hearts sink as sunlight disappears from the sky.
The muddy puddles become larger as it rains down hard.
The streets become uncrowded as people frantically run for shelter.
The cobbled streets are now deserted and silent.
As the precious rain continues to fall.

Sarah Brennan (13)
Icknield High School

ZODIAC

As Pisces the fish swims through the sea
    Capricorn the mountain goat climbs a mountain
As Virgo brushes her long, silky blonde hair
    Gemini share a scoop of ice cream
As Scorpio the scorpion crawls around the desert
    Cancer the crab enjoys life on the beach
As Leo the lion rules the jungle
    Taurus the bull chases people over fields
As Libra the scales weigh the flour
    Aquarius carries her water urn
As Aries the ram eats the green grass
    Sagittarius the half man, half horse
    Shoots arrows with his golden bow.

Gemma Rutherford (12)
Icknield High School

I AM

In the mirror I see a person,
That is supposed to be me,
A human being, with my own identity,
Who am I?
I am a son and a child,
I am a brother,
I am a friend,
I came with these feelings,
When I was born
And these will end when I die.
But not visible is the real me,
For my soul cannot be seen.

Bhavash Karsan (13)
Icknield High School

MY POEM ON ZODIAC

S is for stars that glow in the night.
T ime by time they shine so bright.
A nd help you see in the night.
R eady to hear about your star sign.

S tar signs tell you about yourself.
I n the book the answer is right
to tell you about yourself and your star sign.
G oing left and right
Aries and fairies you will find.
N ow the poem has come to an end.
S tar signs like Leo, Cancer, Aries and Virgo
they are people true star signs.

Kamal Barrie (12)
Icknield High School

HELL ON EARTH

I read my horoscope this week,
I'll tell you the future's looking bleak.
The picture of death, an omen, a sign,
That my life is on the line.
A shell goes screaming overhead,
My friends and I are hiding from lead.
My chance of death, is a bit more,
Being in a war and all.
I dare not stick my head above,
The frozen, war-torn, stinking mud.
I wait and wait for the signal to come,
And when it does, I run and run . . .

Philip Risby (13)
Icknield High School

SELLOTAPE

> It's round and sticky,
> It's used in the office,
> It's round and sticky,
> It's used in the class,
> It's round and sticky,
> It's easy to use,
> It's quick and fast.

See-through and sticky,
It sticks to you,
See-through and sticky,
It's made for you,
See-through and sticky,
It suits what you do.

> It's cheap to make,
> It fixes things which you break,
> Do you know what it is?

It's called Sellotape!

Chris O'Neil (13)
Icknield High School

PERFECTLY STILL

As he stands there perfectly still,
As the world goes on by.
Not a sound,
Not a care,
Standing there perfectly still.

He stands there perfectly still,
Admiring the lovely view.
The wind blowing,
The waves crashing,
He stands there perfectly still.

As he stands there perfectly still,
The sun shining on his spot.
The water glistening,
The beach sands sparkling,
As he stands there perfectly still.

Emma Lambert (13)
Icknield High School

SYMBOLS

Leo is represented by the lion,
Fearsome, brave and strong.
Libra the scales of justice,
Can judge the difference
Between right and wrong.
Pisces the fish swimming in opposite ways.
The Gemini twins showing differences
In their identical gaze.
The Zodiac symbols show their traits.
The animals chosen hereby state;
Taurus the bull, stubborn and tough,
Aries the ram, wise but not rough.
Cancer the crab has a tough shell,
But inside its heart is soft as well.
The scorpion has a sting in its tail,
For those who cross it or fail.
The remaining Zodiac signs,
Virgo the virgin
Capricorn the sea-goat
And Sagittarius the archer,
Conclude the symbols and signs of the Zodiac.

Josh Aarons
Icknield High School

REPTILES

Watch the chameleon if you can,
Not visible to beast nor man.
Lying in the jungle heat,
Devouring all insects he may meet.
Purple, green, red or blue,
Camouflaging itself to hide from you.

Look, a snake slithering across the ground,
You can hardly see it, it makes no sound.
Slithering silently, night and day,
Swallowing whole, its rodent prey.
In the water, on the land,
Snakes to me are very grand.

Alligators and nasty crocs,
Swimming in and out the rocks.
Swiping prey with his killing claws,
Then destroying them with his massive jaws.
When the fishes are silent and still,
He opens his jaws ready to kill.

Scott Courtney (13)
Icknield High School

SPACE!

S   is for the Satellite which configurates the Earth.
P   is for Planets like Pluto and Mars.
A   is for Aliens who try to destroy the Earth.
C   is for Comets which fly around in space.
E   is for the Earth, our planet and our home.

Adil Farooq (11)
Icknield High School

LIFE IS JUST LIFE ...

Life is just life,
It's just another star sign.
Life is just life,
It's just another birthday.
Life is just life,
We just don't care.
Life is just life,
It's just not fair.
Life is just life,
A Chinese new year.
Life is just life,
It's full of plain fear.
Life is just life,
God's new creation.
Life is just life,
It's all just a fascination.

Sarah Heatherwick (12)
Icknield High School

SPIDERS

Spiders quick to get their prey,
Spiders quick to get away.
Spiders in your house and outside,
Spiders ready to eat their fly.
Spiders here and spiders there,
Spiders in your bed, beware!
Spiders eating flies and moths,
Spiders in your kitchen cloths.
Spiders go and spiders come,
Now my spider poem's done.

Edward McDermott (13)
Icknield High School

ELEPHANTS

Elephant, Elephant grey and rough,
With folds of skin that are so tough,
Their great long trunks are so strong
Men killing for their ivory is so wrong.

Who designed something as big as a house?
For a person who's designed a little mouse?
African plains are the best,
For elephants to have a peaceful rest.

They have very large ears,
Do you think they have fears?
Their trunks are very versatile,
When they trumpet you can hear it a mile away.

Elephant, Elephant grey and rough,
With folds of skin that are so tough,
Their great long trunks are so strong
Stop men killing them for their ivory
Because it's so wrong.

Victoria Heywood (13)
Icknield High School

KNOCKOUT

Two brave men, battling for the win,
Taking heavy blows and causing anxiety for one another.
Thinking every punch could be the last.
Struggling to stand,
The red shorts,
Swings his last piece of energy into the blow,
That wins the title.
Knockout.

Ebrahim Parkar (14)
Icknield High School

ZODIAC

Zodiac means many things,
Signs from the sky
That appears every night
Sirius in great dog shining . . .
Shining . . . so bright.

Zodiac means many things,
Pictures in the sky
Great scorpions and fishes
Precious stones of the year,
Opal, amethyst, turquoise, emerald.

Zodiac means many things,
Message in the sky
Telling us the future
When birthdays come around.

Zodiac means many things,
What does it mean to you?

Rebecca Findlay (12)
Icknield High School

THE FIGHT

Two men giving their all
Tired and desperate
One man gives it all up
In one punch
Luckily he hits
The flashes and the crowd go wild
The fight of will and mind
Is over.

Michael Pearson (13)
Icknield High School

THE KING OF THE JUNGLE

I am Leo as brave as can be
all the animals I meet always flee
The king of the jungle is me
don't mess with me you'll see
The loudness of my roar
will make you run out the door
The tiger, panther and snake
never makes me shake
The sharpness of my claws
will surely make you fall to the floor
The glow of my mane
will surely put you to shame
The glare of my stare
will make you fall off your chair
My body is so firm
it makes your stomach churn
So I am Leo
so don't mess with me.

Luke Edgeley (11)
Icknield High School

SNOWFLAKES

Snowflakes falling from the sky
One by one past my eye
They start off high and end up low
That's because they're made of snow

They're white and frozen soft and clear
When they fall we give a cheer
At Christmas time they're never here
So that's why the paths are clear

They're soft and gentle down from the sky
They soar like a bird on the wing flying by
Some are round, some square and flat
I'll help build a snowman big and fat.

Simon Hayes (13)
Icknield High School

STAR SIGN

There are twelve star signs
Pisces is mine
My lucky number is eleven
But I'd much rather prefer seven

My lucky animal is a fish
Which I think looks a dish
There are four elements
And mine is water

My lucky metal is aluminium
Which is very strong
My lucky colour is blue
What about you?

My lucky planet is Neptune
Which is near the moon
I can also see the future through my star sign
I know what is going to happen now
I am going to end my poem.
Bye.

Sabina Haque (12)
Icknield High School

IF ONLY I COULD BE AN ALIEN . . .

If only I could be an alien,
I would get to see all the planets,
It would be great to see the world,
And what it looks like from outside,
It would be great fun.

I would be green and very slimy,
I would have my own ship and my friends,
I would keep servants to do work,
We will rule over planets,
And relax all the time.

If only I could be an alien,
I would get to see all the planets,
It would be great to see the world,
And what it looks like from outside,
It would be great fun.

I would go around and see space,
I would see if there's any new planets,
I would see the beautiful stars,
I would explore on the planets,
And see what's happening.

If only I could be an alien,
I would get to see all the planets,
It would be great to see the world,
And what it looks like from outside,
It would be great fun.

Unfortunately I am not an alien,
How nice it would be to be one,
If only I could be an alien . . .

Jaleela Ahmed (12)
Icknield High School

A Poem For Mums And Dads

A computer was something on TV,
A window was something you hated to clean,
An application was for employment,
A program was a TV show,
A cursor used profanity,
A keyboard was a piano,
Memory was something that you lost with age,
And if you had a 3-inch floppy,
You hoped nobody found out.
Compress was something you did to the garbage,
Not something you did to a file,
And if you unzipped anything in public,
You'd be in jail for a while,
Log on was adding wood to the fire,
Hard drive was a long trip on the road,
A mouse pad was where a mouse lived,
And a backup happened to your commode,
Cut you did with a pocket knife,
Paste you did with glue,
A web was a spider's home,
And a virus was the flu.
I guess I'll stick to my pad and paper,
And the memory in my head,
I hear nobody's been killed in a computer crash,
But when it happens, they'll wish they were dead.

Andy Greaves (13)
Icknield High School

What Star Sign Am I?

Am I a Leo?
Am I a Pisces
Or am I a Taurus?
What star sign am I?
I don't know

Am I a Libra?
Am I a Sagittarius
Or am I a Cancer?
What star sign am I?
I don't know

Am I a Gemini?
Am I a Virgo
Or am I an Aquarius?
I don't know

Am I an Aries?
Am I a Scorpio?
I know
I'm a Capricorn
So now I know.

Hitesh Patel (11)
Icknield High School

Who Am I?

I am like the sea,
Gushing to and fro,
Being dark, deep and mysterious,
Exactly like me.

I am like a rock,
Hard and heavy,
Always stubborn and never moving,
Exactly like me.

I am like a tree,
Swaying in the wind,
Branching into many forms,
Exactly like me.

But better than anything,
Than sea, rock and tree,
Is that I'm an individual person,
Exactly like me.

Umer Hakeem (13)
Icknield High School

ALIENS

Here comes the Zodiac,
He has the front of a car as a chest,
Here comes the Zodiac,
He is simply the best.

Here comes the Zodiac,
He is a bat,
Here comes the Zodiac,
He eats cats.

Here comes the Zodiac,
He sleeps on a mat,
Here comes the Zodiac,
He has a friend which is a rat.

Here comes the Zodiac,
He eats mammals,
Here comes the Zodiac,
He really likes camels.

Lauren Bowyer (11)
Icknield High School

ZODIAC REMINDS ME

Zodiac reminds me of star signs,
My star sign is Gemini,
It reminds me of the Greeks,
Like the one with one eye.

It reminds me of Gladiators,
Zodiac was really strong,
It reminds me of the Ford car,
That used to whiz along.

It reminds me of birthdays,
Mine is in June,
It reminds me of aliens,
Like the one that's like a prune.

It reminds me of Thorpe Park,
It spins round and round,
It reminds me of lightning,
On the Earth it pounds.

It reminds me of Chinese signs,
Horse, pig, tiger and rat,
Dragon, sheep, ox and monkey,
Dog, snake, rooster and rabbit.

Zodiac!

Robin Cooper (11)
Icknield High School

THE ZODIAC

Star signs and birthdays
Are what the Zodiac means to me
Leo, Capricorn, Aries
And I've only mentioned three.

A star sign in the paper
Will say what your future holds,
It's up to you
If you believe what you have been told.

Emily Quince (11)
Icknield High School

ZODIAC

What star sign were you born under?
On which day were you born?
Was it a lovely sunny day?
Or where the skies brewing a storm?
Can the planets dictate the future?
Can the constellations know
If I was born Aquarius, Cancer or Leo?

Do I believe the prediction
Mystic Meg can see for me?
Will it really happen tomorrow?
I'll have to wait and see.
Will I grow up happy?
Will I marry and be a dad?
Will man live on the moon one day?
Is global warming bad?

I'm not sure if my fortune
Can be told by Russell Grant.
Just by being born Aquarius
Does that mean that I'm smart?
If only the gods could tell me
What my future holds.
I think that I'll have to wait and see
What fates will soon unfold.

Lewi Saunders (12)
Icknield High School

THE TWELVE SIGNS OF THE ZODIAC

Scorpios have a sting in their tails,
While Libra stands and holds her scales.
Pisces swims around a moat,
And Capricorn's a lively goat.

Aquarius pours water from a pot,
While Taurus runs riot in a china shop.
Virgo is a lovely lady,
Along with Gemini, the two twin babies.

Leo the lion, crouching low,
Sagittarius kills him with his bow.
The final two are Cancer the crab,
And Aries the ram, who's really fab!

Gemma Hales (12)
Icknield High School

ZODIAC

Zodiac
What is that?

A ride at Thorpe Park
Or some kind of car?

I know, I'm a snake!
But some kind of stone has got to be a mistake!

Perhaps I'm an Aries or a Leo?
Well I don't know!

Zodiac
What is that?

Toby Henness (12)
Icknield High School

TERRIFYING WARRIORS

They're rough and tough
They're fierce and furious
Their shiny armour
Their deadly weapons
Their musty face paint
Their ugly face
Their innermost thoughts
Their innermost feelings
Their bloodshot eyes
But most of all they're terrifying.

Rebecca Ashby (12)
Icknield High School

SPACE, SPACE

Space, space is really cool
And those silly alien fools
The planets are big
With lots of pigs
And those flaming fireballs

Space, space has lots of stars
Even gold glowing stars
The stars are twinkling
While everyone's thinking
What lovely stars they are.

Tanya Blacksley (12)
Icknield High School

ZODIAC

When you are born it's time to celebrate and cheer
But your Zodiac sign is governed by the time of the year
Everyone has a sign dedicated to them
And generally speaking the characteristics are right
Nine times out of ten
With all the twelve signs you cannot pick and choose
It all depends on when you're born whether you win or lose
There's Taurus, Scorpio, Leo, Capricorn, Aries and Pisces
Whose creatures all have tails
Then Sagittarius, Aquarius, Virgo, Gemini, Cancer
And finally Libra the scales
Whichever sign you end up with you can't really complain
Because of the time of your birth
The sign with you will remain.

Katie Olde (13)
Icknield High School

SCORPIO

I was born on the 1st of the 11th '89
Therefore Scorpio is my sign

A Scorpion is my symbol
Which is small, light and nimble

Be careful if you stand and linger
Because I may get you with my stinger

So if this poem's all about me
You might find me under the Zodiac tree.

Tom Connelly (11)
Icknield High School

SPACE

There I was in space
Where I cannot be traced

I see all the asteroids floating
I see all the scientists noting

Space goes on for ever
When will it stop? . . . Never!

Stars in space
What a wondrous place

Comets in space
Hurtling by different places

Will they hit
Or will they miss?

Only space has the answer to this.

Craig Edwards (11)
Icknield High School

ZODIAC

Z odiac is the sign of the stars
O n them you can predict your future
D ay by day you read them
I wonder if they really come true?
A ries is just one of the signs
C ancer is another one too.

Amy Rickman (12)
Icknield High School

THORPE PARK IS FUN

Thorpe Park is fun
It makes you want to run
Because it is exciting you can't wait to get on the rides
Thorpe Park is fun
Especially when your star sign is Libra
You'll be as stripy as a zebra
But all we know is that Thorpe Park keeps you riding
It is fast, colourful and spinning
And it will be also painful
If you make your life so dreadful
So don't make it so regretful
So bear in that in mind
Thorpe Park is *fun!*

Sarah Sackey (12)
Icknield High School

ZODIAC MAKES ME THINK OF . . .

Zodiac makes me think of sporty cars
with steaming engines that go so fast.
Zodiac makes me think of great fighting warriors
with steel golden shields and glazing swords.
Zodiac makes me think of great gods
like Zeus and people who once ruled the world.
When I think of Zodiac I imagine flying deep into space
and through the stars.
And that's why when I hear 'Zodiac'
I imagine me being in a different time and in a different world.

Alex Crawley (11)
Icknield High School

There Is A Monster In Your Basement

There is a monster in your basement
It watches you at night
It's very big and ugly
So it can give you a fright
It's eating all your family
And it's coming up the stars
It's stronger than a whole pack
Of humunguous grizzly bears!
It's getting even closer
You better shut the door
It's gonna get ya soon
You better blow him far away
Just like a big typhoon.

Daniel Johnston (11)
Icknield High School

Zodiac

Here he comes the Zodiac.
The Zodiac is hunting us.
He has teeth like a dragon's
And eyes like an eagle's.
He's hunting us.
We are the last of our kind.
He will find us.
He's hunting us
For fun, for sport?
We do not know.
We run and hide
But he will find us.
He's hunting us till the end.

Kallum Cotcher (12)
Icknield High School

ZODIAC

People read their horoscopes to find out about things like Cupid
But I don't do this, because it's fixed and stupid.
The fate of our future is in our own hands
Not in signs, symbols nor astrological plans.

Your star sign depends on when you were born
Signs include Gemini, Leo and Capricorn.
Taurus the Bull and Aries the Ram
Will tell all about your future, wherever they can.

Cancer the Crab and Pisces the Fish
Are believed to fulfil your every wish.
For money or times to bring you hope
Aquarius and Sagittarius will help you cope.

Virgo the Maiden and Libra the Scales
Joins Scorpio to give a sting to the tale.
Rich or poor, both look to fate
When they look in the newspapers under their date.

David Thomas (12)
Icknield High School

EARTH

The Earth is our planet
The Earth is our home
The sun comes up to warm the Earth
The moon lights up the night sky
Stars shine in the darkness
From light years away

The Earth revolves on its axis
Marking time for a millennium
The tides flow in harmony with the Earth
The Earth is our planet
The Earth is our home.

Caroline Lawson (12)
Icknield High School

ZODIAC

The twins were scared,
With nowhere to go,
They had fled from home,
Into a lonesome night.
Where the silver crescent moon,
Gleamed down on the Earth,
And the magnificent stars,
Glowed like pinpricks in satin.
The twins waded through the sand,
Until they reached the sea,
The children leapt,
And clung onto the silky sky.
They climbed and climbed,
Past the moon, planets and all,
Eventually there came one final place,
A place where they were named Gemini
And remained forever as two little stars,
A place called Zodiac.

Rebecca Witterick (12)
Icknield High School

Zodiac

There are many different stars,
each one brighter than the last,
all twinkling like diamonds,
in the midnight sky.
So in the light of the moon,
you can watch the world go by,
in company of the diamonds.
In a dream I have drifted up to the sky,
and have climbed the diamonds,
that shimmer so bright.
At the very top I sat on one,
I felt as light as a feather,
like an angel in her sleep.
I wished upon a shooting star,
that I could become a diamond,
and my wish came true,
because right at this moment,
I am shining right down on you.
So in this world there are many different stars,
each one as beautiful as *you!*

Rebecca Hendy (11)
Icknield High School

My Dad Is A Cancer

My dad is a Cancer
and on a full moon he goes lairy
He's bright, funny and crazy
and his chest is very hairy.

My mum is a Taurus
and she can be quite weird
Sometimes I worry that
she might start to grow a beard.

My sister is an Aries
and she is so mean
She punches my sister Stevie
but Stevie is so keen

My brother is a Leo
he thinks he's really tough
Everyone knows he's not
because he's not even rough.

Jade Newns (12)
Icknield High School

THE ZODIAC

Are there any signs of a Zodiac?
I have not seen one yet.
I've heard they're big and scary,
I'm sure they are I bet.

I have been told they are spotty,
And have blue on them too.
So keep your eyes wide open,
I hope I've given you a clue.

I am not sure where they're from,
I think they are from Mars.
They must be like an alien,
All they eat is candy bars.

They also eat people,
Be careful what you do.
You don't know its next victim,
It could always be you!

Holly French (11)
Icknield High School

WHAT I WANT FOR MY BIRTHDAY

My birthday is coming
I know what I would like
I don't want a football
Or a whistle
Or a bike
Just a little motor car
It does not have to be new
I'm sure you will agree with me
When you have thought it through
I just want a Mini
I am not insane
But now I have thought it through
'Mum can I have a plane?'

Lisa Curran (12)
Icknield High School

ZODIAC

Zodiac might be the stars
Zodiac could be on Mars
Zodiac could be my cat
It could be what I'm looking at
It could be the roller coaster I went on last week
It could be something I'm going to eat
It could be as simple as a pen
It could even live in my den
Well I guess I've come to the end of that
But if there's more I'll come right back.

Lauren Watson (12)
Icknield High School

ZODIAC

The stars always twinkle so bright.
The stars belong to Heaven or I think they might.
I wish I could climb upon a star.
Oh how I wish they were not so far.
The stars shine silver and are always bright,
They make me feel safe while I'm asleep at night.
The stars appear so small in the sky.
I really wish stars weren't so high.
If I could touch a star right now,
If somebody knows please tell me how.

Charlotte Perrott (11)
Icknield High School

ZODIAC

Zodiac is like a roller coaster
The stars go up and down.

The man on the moon looks down
With his big glass spoon
And yawns as the sun goes down.

As the night creeps over the sky
So do the planets and stars.

If you're lucky at night look up at the sky
And you might see the big white pie.

Elizabeth Burch (12)
Icknield High School

ZODIAC

Zodiac the roller coaster is really cool
Everyone says it rules
If you don't go on it you're a fool
You treat it like a golden jewel.

You may step into the ride
We are warning you now you are in for a scare
So make sure your hair
Does not blow in the air.

You may scream if you like
Or you are going to have a sore throat
Make sure you are not
Sitting next to a goat.

I hope you like the ride
And will come back soon.

Pawandip Bahia (11)
Icknield High School

GREAT BEAR

The Great Bear and its little cub,
Flying through the sky,
Stars and comets everywhere,
Whooshing through the sky,
The bears look so warm and cuddly,
If only I could fly.

Tom Rollins (12)
Icknield High School

SPACE!

Up in space it's a wonderland.
The sky is covered with bright stars.
Imagine, flying bright cars.
Space is a wonderland.

Space is hot, you'll get sun burnt.
The asteroids are there for you to learn.
You can see stars, moons and other bright colours.
Space is a wonderland.

When you see the planet Mars
You'll probably need chocolate bars.
You will definitely go to space for a holiday.
Probably on a school holiday.

Lukhneet Bajwa (12)
Icknield High School

ZODIAC

My dad is a Virgo
he's gentle and kind,
My mum is a Scorpio
with a sting behind.
My two brothers are Pisces
both very fishy,
My other's a ram
he sure is not a lamb.
I am a Gemini
enough love for two,
My mum says one's enough
God bless you.

Kurt Lambert (11)
Icknield High School

MY POEM

As the temperature drops
To zero
And below
Will he put on a scarf?
A super hero.
No.
Thick socks?
A winter coat?
A bobble hat?
None of that.
Just a pair of tights,
Boots,
Underpants
And a thermal vest
To cover his chest.

But the mask?
Don't ask
Why?
Some say it's to hide his
Identity
But I think it's
To keep his nose warm
Who's ever heard of a red-nosed
Super hero?

Rachel Underwood (11)
Icknield High School

SPACE

The vast dark cosmos
seems empty like an old oil drum
and yet there could be life out there
we may not be alone

The stars are specks
they are so far away
but out there somewhere far off
another family and children could be at play.

Paul McSkimming (13)
Icknield High School

STAR SIGNS

Goats and crabs
Lions and mermaids
They are all star signs
But which one is mine?
Fishes and sheep
Scorpions and bulls
How do I find out
Which star sign is mine?
Twins and others
I get confused
How do I find out
Which star sign is mine?
Star signs are different
In so many ways
Different months and
Different days
Yet they are all interesting
In their own way.

Amy Venant (11)
Icknield High School

I Am...

I am not just anyone,
I am me,
I am Jade Thomas,
The best I can be.

My friends call me hardworking,
And often quite loud,
I want to be a barrister,
My parents will be proud.

I play the piano,
Do my grades is my dream,
I know I can do it,
It's not as hard as it seems.

I am a younger sister,
I hope a good mate,
I have a few good mates,
Not many I hate.

I am who I want to be,
I'm special and unique,
I am Jade,
I am Jade,
I am me!

Jade Thomas (13)
Icknield High School

Space Queen

All the planets up there in space
I own them all you know
I visit them an hour each day
Come sun, come rain, come snow.

I ride around up there all day
And go from place to place
Meet up with friends who do the same
And float around in space.

Charlotte Norman (12)
Icknield High School

NIGHT KILLER

Dim moonlight,
Stormy clouds.
Lightning flash,
Thunder crack.
Gloomy darkness,
Dame asleep.
Silence breaking,
Door creaking.
Death closer,
Closer, closer.
Grasp taken,
Eyes open.
Screaming terror,
Bones shattering.
Blood seeping,
Covers stained.
Dim moonlight,
Stormy clouds.
Lifeless, cold,
Death!

Matthew Gascoine (13)
Icknield High School

ZODIAC

Zodiac the mind-blowing ride!
Zodiac is daring
Zodiac is scariest
Zodiac!

Zodiac the mind-blowing ride!
Zodiac wants you
Zodiac will get you
Zodiac!

Zodiac the mind-blowing ride!
Zodiac is a big experience of extremes!
Zodiac will make you cry
Zodiac!

Zodiac the mind-blowing ride!
Zodiac is bad
Zodiac is a thriller ride
Zodiac!

Sam Sherwood (12)
Icknield High School

THE FUNNY FACE FROM OUTER SPACE

There was a woman from outer space
Who had a really funny face
Her name was June
She ate the moon
And now she's the size of a hot air balloon.

Alannah Brennan (13)
Icknield High School

ZODIAC BIRTH SIGNS

Leo the lion roars into summer
Whilst Libra balances the colours of the season autumn.

Taurus rampages into spring
And new creatures are born,
At the other end of the year
Capricorn gets ready to celebrate Christmas and New Year.

Aquarius splashes water into winter,
As well, Pisces is gently swimming into Easter.

Cancer sidles into the warmth of the sea
From the blazing sun.
With her power Virgo gets the teachers into the school spirit
Whilst children are nervous.

Lauren Dinham (11)
Icknield High School

ZODIAC

Glittering stars in the black sky,
lighting the planet that is very high.

The little planet Zodiac has never been found,
because it is so far away from the Earth's ground.

The comets all zoom round and round,
to show everyone this planet should be found.

We won't find it because it got hit,
into a dark, black horrible pit.

It got sucked up and got all crushed,
And all the noise stopped. *Hush, hush.*

Naweed Darr (11)
Icknield High School

ABOUT SPACE AND THE JOURNEY

Spaceman, Spaceman
Blasting off the ground
Making every little sound

Spaceman, Spaceman
Shooting through the air
Twice around the moon and back
But where?

Spaceman, Spaceman
Flying through the skies.
To plant your flag on a planet
Never seen by human eyes.

Spaceman, Spaceman
Flying back to Earth.
Back at home
But it was worth.

Nazish Mehreen (11)
Icknield High School

THE ZODIAC

Stars shining in the deep black sky,
Space rockets zooming by.

The Aliens are invading,
Don't surrender now.

Zap them with your laser gun,
Stab them with a sword.

The Zodiac is coming,
You better be ready.

Chris Michell (11)
Icknield High School

ZODIAC

Swishing and swirling and spinning around
Orbiting Earth without a sound
As it goes slowly past
All the other planets going really fast
Every star is extremely bright
Which helps them twinkle in the night
Rockets launch very fast
They often leave with a mighty blast
The galaxy is really wide
Much bigger than the ocean tide
When you're in space no one can hear
Not even if they're really near
Space, space what a wonderful
    Place!

Joanne Webb (11)
Icknield High School

TREES

Trees are big.
Trees are round and green,
Brown and mostly round.
The leaves fall off and also grow again
In all seasons.
And they are also very useful for wood,
Paper, string, cardboard and floorboard.
So they are also very useful for all these things
So every time you see one
Leave it alone and don't pick its leaves.

Loren Hennessy Leach (12)
Icknield High School

MONTHS

January is cold and it's winter
February, we're settled, still cold and bitter
March, getting a little better, much warmer
April, I tell you one thing, it's cold at dawn
May, what a lovely day, it's my birthday
June, good, it's nice and summer
July, the best time, time to watch Dumb and Dumber
August, August is a big pain
September it can sometimes be lame
October, Hallowe'en, spooky
November, time to play hockey
December, Christmas, funny, I love that.
My Zodiac, there you have it!

Jessica Charles (12)
Icknield High School

PLANETS

How many planets are there?
No one could ever know!
As we know, there are nine main ones.
All different as well.

Mercury - the closest to the sun.
Venus - The rocky planet.
Earth - The planet with living things.
Mars - Hot as fire.
Jupiter - The biggest of them all.
Saturn - The planet with rings.
Uranus - Is made up of gas and ice.
Neptune - The coldest of them all.
Pluto - The smallest of them all.

Jessica Fisher (12)
Icknield High School

UNDESERVING

Lethal is the fang of the cobra
as it injects a deadly dose of venom into your bloodstream.
Lethal is the bit of the mosquito
as it gives you malaria.
Lethal are the jaws of the great white shark
as they clamp around your body, piercing your skin.
Lethal are the tentacles of the box jellyfish
as they scrape you causing unbearable pain.
Lethal is time itself,
counting down the seconds until you are too old to carry on.
But none of these things kill for no reason, only the human does that.
God made us the master race and some of us don't deserve that.

Thomas Kelby (12)
Icknield High School

MY BIRTHDAY

When I wake up that morning, when my eyes wake up
I see shiny faces like my mum, my dad and my sister
And *presents* just for me!
Blue ones, red ones, yellow ones
All just for me.
I tear and shred and bite.
Later on a bang on the door, my mates are smiling at me
And I said, 'What presents have you got for me?'
Then we go to Queasier and at the end I feel so sad
Because I have to wait for another year.

Elliott Fensome (12)
Icknield High School

THE ANIMALS OF THE EARTH

I start my journey here,
Monkeys everywhere.
There's a snake near a lake,
And everybody's here.

There's a lion in my shoe,
And a kangaroo in a canoe.
There's a bear with a hare,
And it's eating a pear.

There's a jaguar with a stare,
And a bear without a care.
There's a camel with a hump,
And a bird with a lump.

There's a gorilla with a pillar,
And a silverback and he's called a gorilla.
There's a puffin with a muffin,
And a fish with a fin that went for a swim.

There's a spider with a web,
And an ant with an egg.
The wildebeest run so fast,
And the antelope graze on the grass.

The giraffe is so tall,
It makes me look small.
The crocodile has sharp teeth,
And it called Bonjovie Keith.

An ostrich has very long legs,
And lays very, very large eggs.
There's a rhino called Dino,
And likes to eat lino.

Sarah White (12)
Icknield High School

I Can Be...

I can be... famous
I can be a movie star
I can travel near and far
I can be a cover girl
I can sing, dance and twirl

I can be... brave
I can be in the fire force
I can save lives by taking a course
I can be a doctor or nurse
Stop people from needing to ride in a hearse

I can be... caring
I can be a high school teacher
I can help children like a preacher
I can work in social care
Be proud of the kids and that they've got somewhere

I can be... at the top
Be the big cheese boss
I can be happy and get cross
I can look down on lots of people
Or I won't because we could be equal

I can be... what I want
I can do what I want to do
I can work outside or at home too
I don't know what I will be
But I know that no mater what I will
... Be me.

Kathryn Rouse (13)
Icknield High School

CANDLE FIRE

See the candle fire and crowd around,
A beautiful, intense flame,
A wonderful and lonely sound,
There's nothing quite the same.

She breaths a black, smoggy breath,
And gives people an amazing jab;
She throws a gloomy touch of death,
And sometimes makes you feel quite drab.

When she starts to die out,
Don't be afraid,
But don't give her too much doubt,
As she may still invade.

Menal Katechia (13)
Icknield High School

VAMPIRE

With a great beat of wings, he swooped
Towards me, a swirling dark circle of fright,
I stared, speechless,
My limbs betray me.

His hypnotic eyes led me to despair,
He wrapped his animal arms tightly around,
Slowly he bends his crooked neck,
My throat parched.

His teeth glint, then pierce my flesh,
Blood pours from my ruptured veins,
My body now drained,
The last spark just went out.

Laura Yaxley (14)
Icknield High School

Zodiac's

Today is Zodiac's day,
We are going to buy presents today,
He likes moving stuff like roller coasters and planets,
He went to the roller coaster that goes round and down,
It is so scary but it seems he likes it.
Then we moved to the space rocket,
The speed of G-Force 1
My face was like a monkey,
And Zodiac starting laughing.
We were in space and landed on the moon,
It was beautiful.
Zodiac started crying.
I grabbed a star and I gave it to him
And he kissed me.

Saminah Begum (11)
Icknield High School

My Cats

I have a cat that's as black as night
He can give you quite a fright
My other cat is white and grey
He causes trouble every day
My ginger and white cat is very keen
On washing all day and keeping clean
My three cats are soft and silky to touch
I love them all very much.

Chris Cordwell (13)
Icknield High School

Under My Bed!

There's something under my bed
That spooks me out
Whenever I go to bed
I go with the light on
I think there's something under there
A monster or a bogey man
It might be a pop star
Like Britney Spears
Or my brother and sister
Playing a joke on me
I can see a shadow coming close to me
It looks like a zombie trying to kill me
But I can't see a thing
Coming close to me
No, a zombie!
Hey, don't eat me!

Imran Ahmed (12)
Icknield High School

Planets

All the planets, different sizes,
All the planets, different colours,
Mercury, Venus, Earth and Mars,
Jupiter, Saturn, Uranus too,
Neptune and Pluto, that's the lot,
Of course the sun and moon are great,
Not forgetting all the stars,
Altogether great or small,
All for one and one for all.

Chris Kingshott (11)
Icknield High School

SCHOOL LIFE

'Don't be late,'
Says your mum
'Don't be late,'
Says your dad
'Be on time,'
Says the dog
'Be on time,'
Says the cat
But the clock says, 'You're late,'
As you reach the school gate

Scribble, scribble 100 times
Scribble, scribble just in time
Scribble, scribble don't be late
Scribble, scribble at the school gate.

Adam Dodds (12)
Icknield High School

HAVE YOU EVER SEEN . . .

Have you ever seen an elephant drive?
Have you ever seen a rat skydive?

Have you ever seen a giraffe sing?
Have you ever seen a cheetah swim?

Have you ever seen what presents an ant brings?
No I don't think you've ever seen these things.

Matthew Harvey (12)
Icknield High School

WHY DO ANIMALS SUFFER?

Why do animals suffer?
There's no real reason why
People kick, punch and dump them
Until they whimper, cry or die.

Animals being beaten
And locked up in tiny cages
No space to move or even lay down
And left there forgotten for ages.

Animal testing is equally wrong
Animals crying and pleading out in vain
In little hope that someone will come
And free them from this horrible pain.

Humans shouldn't get away with this
It's nowhere near fair
Animals have feelings too you know
I think more people should care.

Stacey Marum (12)
Icknield High School

PROUD TO BE ME!

Talkative and fun-loving that is me,
Always singing and buzzing like a bee,
I'm always willing, gentle and fun,
Some people say I look like my mum,
I have some friends, Amy and Prue,
Somehow I'll stay honest and true.

Laura Golding (11)
Icknield High School

My Two Loyal Friends

My first is liver and white,
and he sleeps all through the night.
My second is four months old with coal black fur,
his life at the moment is one big blur.

All day they play, jump and bound,
and then after school to the field they go
where they leap around and around.

All they need from me is attention and food,
and they always give me love, even in my darkest mood.
Then they jump up and give me a lick,
and my mood is lifted in a tick.

Ross Colbert (12)
Icknield High School

Pisces

February, Pisces the time I was born,
They never wake up at the crack of dawn!
Swimming through the sea at tremendous speed,
The water, the blue is what they need.
They help and support other people,
Without the help of a steeple.
20th of February to the 20th of March,
The seaweed around turns into an arch.
The kind and friendly fish swimming in the sea,
That's all I ever want to be.

Mark Morris (11)
Icknield High School

MY CATS

My two cats are born to laze,
In the dark,
In the sun,
Or even in the shade.

The eldest named Buttons,
Is slower by far,
But her fun day is chasing Zippy,
And climbing the trees.

The young one called Zippy,
Runs and jumps and plays, with the leaves,
She chases her tail,
And gets in a spin,
Nobody knows what trouble she will get in!

Hannah Gormley (12)
Icknield High School

MY FAMILY!

My mum is great!
I love her so much!
I don't care if she is thirty-eight!
Even though she shouts and screams at me so much.

Pamela is very crazy
Sometimes all she thinks about is her hair.
Also Pamela is most of the time one hundred percent lazy
But I don't care.

My dad works hard
And he is also in charge.
There is nothing else to say about him.

Sally-Anne Wright (12)
Icknield High School

FAME

Fame is glory
Fame is glamour
Fame is hard
Fame is a goal

Fame is short
Fame is long
Fame is sparkle
Fame is a reward

Fame is the top
Fame is high
Fame is low
Fame is fame
    Fame
Fame
    Fame . . .

Lauren Randall (13)
Icknield High School

FARM

I wake in the morning
The cock crows thrice
Now I eat my breakfast, ever so nice
Bring out the horses infected with lice
I saw the mice on the stair
Eating at my underwear
I followed them to their little lair
Then I heard a rip and a tear
But they are not there.

Michael Turner (11)
Icknield High School

A Day In The Life Of Me

I open my eyes,
I see a light.
I get out of bed,
With my entire might.
I put on some clothes,
And walk down the stairs.
I'm wearing a green top,
With blue flares.
I grab an apple,
As for breakfast I will miss.
This apple looks good,
So I'll just have this.
I see Nyalah,
She's really cool.
Our first lesson's PE
I think it rules!
Leigh-Anne is my partner,
As she chucks fifty balls.
I move from side to side,
And catch them all.
As it is a half day,
I only have one class,
But at lunch playing football,
I broke one school glass.
I walk home with Lee, James and Hannah,
All of them turn off.
I'm walking home by myself,
As I start to cough.
I collapse on my bed;
And play a game.
But tomorrow I have
To go to school again.

Cassandra Thomas (11)
Icknield High School

MY ANIMALS

I've got a rabbit,
Which has lovely, long, floppy ears,
I've got a rabbit,
That looks so lovely.

I've got a rabbit,
Which has lovely, soft, brown fur,
I have a rabbit
That looks so lovely.

I've got a dog
Which has lovely, nice, brown eyes
I have a dog
That looks so lovely.

I've got a dog
Which has lovely and soft, spotty fur,
I have a dog
Which looks so lovely.

I have a cat
Which has lovely, pointed ears,
I have a cat
That looks so nice.

I have a cat
Which is very shy but playful,
I have a cat
That looks so nice.

Dipa Tailor (12)
Icknield High School

ZODIAC

Here I am standing in the zone
Where I stand all alone,
Here the crystal
Telling secrets all alone,
Here are Pisces
Swimming all alone,
Here are the scorpions
Cracking their pincers
All alone
Here comes the moon
Cracking the light all alone
Here comes Mystic Meg
All alone,
Here comes the palm
All alone,
Here come
Peace and love
With all
Here comes
The sun shining
All around,
Here comes
The stars
As shiny as can be,
Here comes
Star cards,
Flying all around,
Here comes everyone,
Coming to work.

Luke Firth (11)
Icknield High School

A Wonderful World!

O world full of wonders
O world full of might
Approach not this naive soul
Tempt not me, with delight
For your plentiful ease
Will most certainly cease
And put out your temporary light.

O world full of glitter!
O world full of gold!
Get away from my presence
Before you are told
For your enchanting call
Will not lead me to fall
In my hand, a strong rope, I hold.

O world full of comfort!
O world full of charm!
I see you as a dungeon
Disguising your harm
But amidst your tribulation
Is a gateway to salvation
God's straight path of purity and calm.

O world! Be no distraction
From meaning Acton
This young slave seeks some time -
More true to leave me alone peacefully
My Lord - I shall serve willingly
O next life! My soul yearns for you.

Amer Javed (12)
Icknield High School

My Best Friend Is Truly Amazing!

My best friend is . . .

B ubbly
E nthusiastic
S miley
T rying hard, always to care for others

F riendly
R eassuring
I s willing to help, always with a smile
E xciting
N icola De Ronde
D aring.

Michaela Reid-Thomas (11)
Icknield High School

Sagittarius

S aturn, an angry red
A wesome guy
G reat person
I know what's best
T ries his best
T ime, they are always late
A gree, should or shouldn't?
R ich in the head
I dea well sent
U nique in every way
S agittarius the best and the kindest.

Jai Tailor (11)
Icknield High School

COLA BOTTLE

C olliding with my teeth it leaves them numb,
O h why does it tickle on my tongue?
L uxury at its max but price at the minimum,
A nd it also comes with crystals which tingle in your mouth,

B eware though it can become gooey and sticky,
O n the whole it's the best delight,
T hat could be eaten,
T onight,
L ingering around in your mouth it tastes
E xceedingly good.

Manjit Sobti (12)
Icknield High School

COLA BOTTLE

C lear on the inside when you bite into it
O val is its shape
L ooks so tantalising
A bsolutely nothing could taste as good

B etter the cola bottle that's eaten, not me
O nly if I could eat them all the time
T ickling my throat all the way down
T angy and sweet it was
L ovely and delicious it was tasting
E lastic and stretchy.

Dominic Carrick (13)
Icknield High School

SHADOWS CREEP BY

All alone in fear-breathing territory
I hear shrieks and shouts in eerie harmony
Glancing around in a dark dreary web
The spider has caught me I fear I am dead
Swirling around like a whirlpool of death
His hands hugged my neck, I dare to dread
He says, 'One bit of this fair neck'
As blood droplets echo
One sharp stab with a stake
He will not wake
That's the end, his sharp teeth sank
Like a fish, I've floated to the top of the tank
He runs, he hides down deep into darkness
I lie peacefully
As
Shadows creep by.

Natalie McPhee (13)
Icknield High School

MY TASTY CHERRY-COLA BOTTLE

This nice and colourful sweet
Is wonderful, ripe and ready to eat.
This sweet is so unique,
You could not
Mistake if for some hairy, smelly feet.
When you put it in your mouth
And your taste buds arise,
Then they think, what a wonderful surprise!

Yasmin Rose (11)
Icknield High School

My Grandma Thinks She Can Read Tea Leaves

Grandma was sitting by her tea mug,
'It's a bad omen,' she said,
'The Star Gods, they are angry,
I felt it early morning, while I was sitting in my bed.'

'Sure you did Grandma, that's what you always say.'
'I *can* read tea leaves,' she moaned.
Then I sighed and walked away,
Suddenly she gasped, so I ran in the room,

'The tea leaves never lie!' she exclaimed,
Then drank up all her tea.
'Oh, it's very grave news,' she cried
'You do not believe me.'

Phillippa Gray (11)
Icknield High School

Fear!

When you feel fear you tingle from head to toe,
Something inside which makes your burn go.
You feel so scared, frightened and lost,
The rate ain't money, death is the cost.

Your head filled with scary thoughts and dreams,
All you can imagine, torture and scream.
Devils and demons, ghosts in your mind,
The Grim Reaper grinding his teeth from behind.

Your heart beating so loud there's an earthquake,
You look in the mirror, your body's opaque.
Your worst nightmare is coming alive,
The word fear soon will arrive.

Rebecca Mathurin (12)
Icknield High School

A FLYING SAUCER

Tingled my tongue when I first took a bit.
It's round and smooth at first sight.
You shake it
And break it
And out pours a sugary delight.

It's smooth on top
And rough around.
There's no pop
And no other sound.

Tingled my tongue when I first took a bit.
It's round and smooth at first sight.
You shake it
And break it
And out pours a sugary delight.

There's something about it,
Which makes you think.
What is it?
The colour is pink?

Tingled my tongue when I first took a bite.
It's round and smooth at first sight.
You shake it
And break it
And out pours a sugary delight.

Gurpreet Chattha (12)
Icknield High School

A SWEET SWEET

The sweet was wrapped in a white crunchy wrapper,
It was a very bright pink,
It was as hard as a wall,
In the middle was a liquidy pink liquid.

When I unwrapped the crunchy white wrapper,
I put it in my mouth,
It tasted very sour,
Very much the liquid, it was most sour.

Michaela Blake (11)
Icknield High School

Winter Fun

I ran down the stairs
    with a grin on my face
As I looked out the window
    snow drifted like lace
As I ran for the door
    I grabbed hold my coat
Then I did up the buttons
    right up to my throat

I picked up some snow
    and rolled out a ball
Then I made a large snowman
    he was ever so tall
I picked up two stones
    and made them his eyes
Then I broke off some branches
    and made him a tie

The snow became chilly
    so I raced to the door
I sat by the fire
    and dozed on the floor.

Amey White (12)
Icknield High School

I Went To A Spooky Castle

I went to a spooky castle
To deliver a fragile parcel,
I went up the steps
And rang the bell,
In a gust of wind I heard a yell,
A green, slimy slug answered the door,
I looked behind him and there was a big
Slimy trail left on the floor,
So I gave him the parcel
And unlucky for me,
The slug asked me into the castle,
So I went in the room
And there in a cage were baboons,
So I turned around
And ran from the castle,
That's what happened to me
When I delivered
To a spooky castle.

Callum Symonds (12)
Icknield High School

My Poem

The sweet I tried was very sour,
It was also very soft.
The sweet I tried was very sugary,
The sweet I had, had jelly inside,
It was also split into different flavours,
The sweet I had was cherry and coke flavour
And it was very stretchy.

The sweet I tried was pink,
It was also very sour.
The sweet was shaped like a flying saucer,
The sweet was very smooth on the outside,
It was very fizzy on the inside,
The sweet also rattled
And the sweet was round.

Katie Yau (11)
Icknield High School

VAMPIRE

His mad eyes shone bright
on his chalky face,
with waxen skin stretched taught.
His breath was a death rattle
sucking life from the thick air.

He pounced
and with tapered digits
wrapped himself around my neck
like a hideous travesty of a scarf.

My body was heavy, so heavy
and my mind was stretched
round a thousand pins
and slowly I sank, into the
stagnant pool of death.

Amy Haggett (13)
Icknield High School

MY BEST FRIEND IS A . . .

My best friend is an animal, she eats her body parts,
First her fingers, then her toes and
Then for dessert she eats her nose.

My best friend is an alien,
At school she failed to shine,
But no matter how clever,
No matter how dumb,
That alien will always be mine.

My best friend is my sister,
She's my bestest friend,
But even though she's only 1,
This friendship will never end.

Sam Gower (11)
Icknield High School

MY POEM

The sweet is very sour
You look at every hour

You suck it and suck it
Until it wears away

It smells of lemon
And a bitter taste of Heaven

You still suck it
Until it goes away.

Carl Jolley (11)
Icknield High School

I WANT TO BE A STAR!

I want to be a star,
I want to drive a Jaguar,
I want to go far,
Not just have coppers in a jar.

I want to see myself on the TV screen
And make the cover of a magazine,
I want to meet Mr Bean
And be in a pop group called *Steam*.

I want to make a chocolate kite
And eat it up in one big bite,
I want to see my name in lights
And be known by everyone in sight.

I want to be a star,
I want to drive a Jaguar,
I want to go far,
But I'm only predicted to work in a burger bar!

Nicola Peet (12)
Icknield High School

COLA

Fizzy, chewy, sweet,
Tasting sweet and sour,
If you get it on your feet
You will have lots of power.
Inside it looks like jelly
And if you eat a lot of these
You will have a big belly.

Raymond Poon (12)
Icknield High School

PISCES

Pisces are the best,
In the world simply better than the rest,
Pisces rule,
They're so cool,
That's why they're the best.

Pisces are fish,
They aren't a dish,
They've got personality,
They've got originality,
This is they way I want to be.

If you haven't guessed yet,
You better go out and get,
'Cause I bet,
Pisces are the best.

Dominic Williams (11)
Icknield High School

HOLIDAY

Today's the day I'm going on holiday,
Away from my teachers, away from my house.
I'm going to Majorca, it's gonna be fun,
I'm going with my dad and mum.
I'll go the beach and have a swim,
I'll go to discos to boogie and sing.
I'll go to the shops and buy lots of toys,
I'll also chat up lots of cute boys.
But now it's time to get on that plane,
To go and enjoy a summer holiday.

Joanne Arnold (12)
Icknield High School

WINTER

Winter is cold,
Winter is freezing,
Winter is frost,
Winter is the home of snow.

Snow falls gently to the ground,
Covering the world with white ice,
Make snowmen in winter,
Have a snowball fight.

Winter is fun,
Everyone loves winter,
You will get presents in the middle of winter,
You get to do all the best things in winter.
Winter is the best.

Hassan Abu (11)
Icknield High School

DRACULA

D ead, he leaves you pale and white,
R ed, his mouth from sucking your blood
A nimal, he turns and leaves you decomposing
C offin, he sleeps until he wakes from the dead
U nderground, his lair heaves with bats
L ate, at the dead of midnight he smells his meal is near
A gain, he takes another life, not knowing who will be next.

Christopher Growestock (13)
Icknield High School

My Best Friend

My best friend is caring and kind,
She is very generous to a guy,
She never tries to lie,
Whenever people put her down and hurt her, she starts to cry.
She is very sensitive to this guy,
She will do anything for him,
Even though he's a bit dim.
He's a pain in the neck but she still fancies him,
But he don't fancy her,
He fancies me.
His name is Aaron, he's a bit of a pain but who ain't?
She invites me to her house sometimes,
But all she talks about is Aaron.
She talks about how she looks and sounds,
She has blonde hair, blue eyes, quite small.
If you have not guessed by now, then you'll never know.
Here is a clue just to help,
She is in 8Y5, Mrs Booth,
She is good friends with Sarah Dill,
Come on, you must know now.
Laters.

Kylie-Marie Clarke (12)
Icknield High School

Aries

A ssociated with war and combat!
R uled by Mars.
I have a sharp temper, apparently and am
E xtremely selfish sometimes!
S ymbol is a ram, that's what makes Aries the *best!*

David Millard (11)
Icknield High School

MORNING MONSTER

This morning at breakfast
When I cracked my egg,
A monster jumped out
With a hairy leg.
I'm telling you straight
(And it ain't no joke,)
He was small and fierce
And covered in yolk.
Well, he stood quite still
And he looked at me,
Then he washed himself
In my cup of tea.
He dried himself
With the morning post
And helped himself
To my piece of toast.
He hit me with a bat,
Like an ant hitting a rat.
He went in the night,
Leaving the house
As a bad sight.

Waseem Ayub (12)
Icknield High School

CAPRICORN

Capricorn is for the pale blue birthstone,
It is a very talkative person - I am
And very funny too.
Capricorn is for the person I am
And very helpful too.

Emma Aylott (12)
Icknield High School

SPACE INVASION

We're under attack, we're under attack
From the giant over there
Come on men, fly west through the air
To our planet we must get back

Oh no! The force is too strong
We're gonna die, we're gonna die, say so long
We're getting crushed by some mighty force
We're in a mouth, I hope this isn't a horse

We're soaked, we've landed in a giant river
Whoosh, we're heading down a great black hole
Back there, back there, is that the liver?
I think I can smell a piece of bread roll

Oh no! We're on the move, getting cramped together with stinky food
Hanging above a great big bowl
Something's head is sticking out like a mole
Urrhh, there is something down the toilet, its name can be rude!

Nathaniel Quigley (12)
Icknield High School

WINTER

Winter is the time we all love,
The snow is the colour of a dove,
As you get in your sledge
You go down a little ledge,
The snow settles on the floor,
It's higher than my door,
As you run into the snow
You look like a piece of dough.

Michael Pridmore (12)
Icknield High School

Dom

My best friend is cool
My best friend is fantastic
My best friend is clever
He is the best ever

My best friend has a red car
My best friend is a football player
My best friend is clever
He is the best ever

My best friend can play any sport
My best friend can play with ease and accuracy
My best friend is clever
He is the best ever

We play together
Whenever we're together
My best friend is clever
He is the best ever

Oh, by the way
My best friend is Dom.

Martin Wood (12)
Icknield High School

Libras

L   is for loveable, a speciality of the Libras
I   is for intelligence and Libras have plenty of that
B   is for blue, colour of the birthstone and the colour of the sea
R   is for reliable, you can always rely on a Libra
A   is for advice, Libra's always have time to talk.

Katerina Drimussis (12)
Icknield High School

MYSELF!

J olly
A thletic
M arvellous
E nergetic
S porty

F unny
A rgumentative
L ovely
C ourageous
'O rrible
N aughty
E nthusiastic
R ude.

James Falconer (12)
Icknield High School

MY POEM

I can see bare trees,
but no bees.
Children with winter hats,
stepping on winter mats.
I can feel the cold,
it smells like gold.
Falling snowflakes,
freezing lakes.
While the snow
lays low
making big mounds of it.
You can see warm fires being lit
and small children learning to knit.

Casie Eldridge (11)
Icknield High School

CANCERIANS

Cancerians are happy, kind and caring
Cancerians are sharing people, fish of the underworld
Cancerians are the lords of fish like the crab with its amazing pincers.

Rachael Anderson (11)
Icknield High School

I GIVE YOU A CRYSTAL

I give you a crystal
For this I can see you through
And on the other side, there you will see me
But don't give it away because it is a token of my love

I give you this crystal
It has been in the family for years
I give it to you because of my love
And hope you take good care of it

I give you a crystal
It can be rough
Just like our rows sometimes
It can be smooth
Like when everything is fine

I give you this crystal
So that you will cherish and love it forever
Every time you look at it
It will remind you of me
Do not lose it
For our love will never be anymore.

Victoria Wilson (14)
Lealands High School

THE REALISATION OF OUR PRESENTATION

What these children need is dedication
A little bit of love and some concentration
To give them some help with their education
Abusing a child is an abomination.

It causes hurt and much frustration
Some children are scared to make the accusation
But all they need is some collaboration
That's the whole meaning of this presentation

What we need is analisation
A little bit of help and evaluation
So we can work together and aid the world nation
So come along and stop this tribulation.

Child abuse is on the multiplication
Fist to mouth without hesitation
Let's help these children, it's our obligation
And when we're done, we can have a celebration.

Nicola Theodore (13)
Lealands High School

DEATH

It is dark, cold and black
How horrible, how sad
Is there a way to get back?
I don't think so, it's driving me mad

This cursed world, which I am in
Some funny creatures which haunt me
I'd rather be in a rubbish bin
Than in this place which no one can see

I am bold
I am strong
I'm not cold
Is something wrong?

So this is death, so this is death
The end of my life, my last breath.

Paul Barnard (14)
Lealands High School

MY CHILDHOOD

My life began as a foetus
Inside my mother's womb.
Listening, wondering, trying to suss
This multicoloured gloom.

At last I had arrived
With all these sounds around.
But I felt so deprived
Like there was no one around.

Toddler life was great
I got lots of dolls and toys.
Then I went to school
And met lots of girls and boys.

Now I'm in year ten
And I'd love to go back again.

Kylie Large (14)
Lealands High School

DEATH

Not a lily, or a rose,
But to your grave, I give a 50 pence piece

It is your life
Bright, bold and silky,
Made in a certain year.
It goes from place to place
And is worth something
To a lot of people.
Just like you.

But soon, this lovely thing
Will turn foggy and grey
And like you,
Its life will extinguish,
Like a crunched-up leaf,
Still and rusty.
Just like you.

Not a lily, or a rose,
But to your grave, I give a 50 pence piece.

Danielle Rosson (13)
Lealands High School

THE MEEK

The meek are so poor,
Unwealthy, unhealthy.

The meek are so ill,
Plagued by disease.

The rich people stare and gaze
And drop a few coppers in their lap.

The meek just ponder,
On what to spend it on.

The meek have no food,
Starved from poverty.

But blessed are the meek,
For they shall inherit the earth.

***Chris Clarke (12)
Lealands High School***

THE THRILL OF IT!

The thrill of it, the thrill of it,
Myself, my bike, my freedom,
I put on my helmet, a perfect fit,
I kick my bike, my freedom.

I love going on my bike,
Especially at weekends,
With all the people that I like,
My dad, my brother, my friends.

Click into gear,
Who could ask for more,
I love to hear
The engine roar.

Zooming on my motorbike,
There's nothing better that I like.

***Christopher Gallagher (14)
Lealands High School***

MY SONNET ON LOVE

My name is Karen, Karen Kontoh,
I have a crush on a boy, he is so fine.
His name is . . . ahh, I'm not going to tell you,
Man, he's so fine, fine, fine.
He has blond hair and blue eyes,
Mr Lover has a face as sweet as roses.
With a yellow bag and a blue coat,
I wish he sent me some roses.
I wish he knew my passion for him,
He has a girlfriend, now what a shame,
The passion in his eyes is like a Friday afternoon.
I just have to shame the girl and her name,
So long my love,
We shall meet my love again.

Karen Kontoh (14)
Lealands High School

THE MAD HATTER

There was a mad hatter
Whose name was called Platter
Who didn't know what to do
So he hired a boat
And left his coat then sailed off to sea
Now deep in the sea
Where people grew free
He met a young lady named Anne
Where they grew up together
And got married whenever
Then cried till their hearts were content.

Jade Goodman (11)
Lealands High School

I Shall Ask Her

I shall ask her, I shall ask her
The way she runs
He big bold smile, the way her hair blows in the wind
Her sweet smell sense
I shall ask her, when the time is ready
The way she makes me blush
The way she calls me Freddy
She's always been my crush
I must let her know I love her
I shall ask her to hear her voice
Her nice blue eyes
Her skin is so moist
I shall ask her, I shall ask her
To ease my pain and let my love free.

Marlon Johnson (15)
Lealands High School

Feelings

Joy, flying in the sky.
Fear, stomping slowly by.
Happiness, filling you with glee,
Anger, stinging like a bee.
Hope, making you feel better,
I can't describe it in a letter.
Relaxation spreads with ease,
Bad mood. Oh no! Help me please!
All these feelings, hard to hide,
Some of them hurt more, deep inside.

Amy Fordham (12)
Lealands High School

LUNCH

The cute kitten,
the moving fur-ball
is sleeping by the fire
inside the silent house.

She awakes,
she walks slowly
over to the sofa,
she purrs -
listening.

With her small
slit-window eyes,
she spies carefully
upon her prey.

With a squeak,
the frightened little mouse
runs towards the comfort
of his hole,
tail trailing behind him.

As the kitten pounces,
the mouse squeals loudly,
she gives the creature
a nasty bite.
Drawing the beautiful
snow-white mouse
closer to his dreadful fate.
Wonderful
lunch at last!

Katherine Hannah Woollard (11)
Lealands High School

FROST

Patiently waiting for darkness to come
She lurks in the shadows.
Staying in her hiding place - not moving
Loneliest of widows.

Night's darkness comes, she goes out to play
Dancing in the soft moonlight,
She spreads her cold, frosty fingertips
And sets a house in her sights.

Flying over frosty fields and silent trees
She lands at the house.
Then she spreads her white, long fingers
As quiet as a mouse.

She flies away to more people's homes
Doing the same again and again
Leaving her mark on the windows
A sparkly ice pattern - never the same.

When that job is done, no time to spare
She wanders over meadows,
She leaves her trail behind again
And slinks back to the shadows.

Spiders in their webs try to copy
The fineness of her designs,
The songbirds in the morning clear
Sing about her fading lines.

So if you see these intricate patterns
By the light of day,
You will know the widow was there
She played and ran away.

Jasmine Pughe (11)
Leighton Middle School

Monster Or Not?

'We're very near!' yelled Jim the climber,
To his coughing companion beside him.
'I know, but don't shout,' Anthony cried,
His wheezing up to the brim.

Their voices echoed round the mountain,
Disturbing the sparkling snow.
Slowly it began to crumble
And downwards it started to flow.

'Now look what you've done,' sneezed Anthony,
As he pointed to a white sheet coming down.
'Well, goodbye then,' Jim said,
As his friend sent his eyebrows to a frown.

A monster pondered over the two unconscious men
And sighed a deep, heavy moan.
'Oh God, not another group of climbers –
Do they understand this is a man-free zone?'

The brown, hairy creature heaved them onto his back,
And carried them to his cave.
'Suppose I'd better rescue them,' he groaned,
'But when they go, I bet they won't even wave.'

With his huge, lumbering feet,
And brown, matted hair;
He has a sweet and gentle nature,
But a dark and menacing stare.

After the screaming and whimpering had stopped,
For the climbers had come across several shocks:
As the yeti explained his predicament,
While they sat by the fire, drying their socks.

The yeti and climbers shook hands and agreed
That they would never again stray.
A promise made for saving two lives -
Other people would laugh anyway.

Jessica Clough (11)
Leighton Middle School

CLOUDS

Have you ever stopped to think,
Why the earth and sky do link?
It is the clouds, as they float by,
Glide across the evening sky.

But who controls these lovely things,
As they float as if on wings?
It is the cloud man, perched up high,
Sitting jauntily in the sky.

Did you ever think you knew,
Though the sky is often blue,
Did you ever stop to think,
They're always grey, hardly pink?

Only for a little while
As the sun falls, mile by mile,
As it dies, ends its sink
The clouds are no longer pink.

I often wonder while asleep,
Then I look, outside I peep,
It's something that we'll never know,
Why he hates the pinkish glow.

Elizabeth Daniels (11)
Leighton Middle School

SHADOW

I lie in bed, awake at night
With my quilt up to my chin
I shiver, faintly cold with fright
A nightmare about to begin.

I see a shadow on my wall
Full of darkness and doom
I cannot sleep, not at all
Suspense is filling my room.

The shadow moving, becomes clearer
It looks thin and daunting
It's closing in, coming nearer
It feels extremely haunting.

Silence makes the room so tense
My head is full of questions
Nothing now is making sense
The shadow gives suggestions.

The shadow now is taking shape
It's becoming crisper
All I can do is sit and gape
There's no sound – not a whisper.

I know what the shadow's supposed to be
Of course it is a finger
It's telling me to hurry, hurry
And of course not to linger.

It's shouting at me very loud
I dare not even peep
It's telling me to do it now
'Go on, go to sleep!'

Maudie Wyatt (11)
Leighton Middle School

NOISE IN THE NIGHT!

It was midnight on the Devon moors
And in a tent with canvas floors,
Sat one girl who bravely slept alone,
Except she wasn't on her own.

She with a start awoke to hear
A flapping sound that met her ear.
She listened for a time unknown
And heard something that gave a moan.

But now she was convinced that there
Was something out there that would tear
Her flesh apart,
She felt the beating of her heart . . .

Until the tension was too great,
She unzipped the tent to seal her fate.
The gruesome thing that met her eyes,
Was something of a big surprise.

For there was silence on the moors;
She could see no gruesome claws.
Her imagination had run wild,
She'd scared herself to death, poor child.

But one thing that will come of this:
She's sharing with her little sis.

Lucy Williamson (11)
Leighton Middle School

THE WILD WHITE HORSES

I swam out into the deep blue sea,
Where nobody could see me.
The sun was hot and shining but,
The waves were beating down.

The wild white horses were crashing
All around me, rumbling, braying, neighing.
Their manes of foam were flying as they rode across the sea.

I saw the jellyfish swim past, so white, so pure,
I saw the swarms of angelfish rush past me,
I saw the shark gaining on me.

I saw the yachts floating before me;
I was even further out than them,
I saw the ferries out before me, I'm not that far out.

I felt my energy leaking out through my body,
Out into the fish; out into the boats; out into the sea.
The wild white horses stampeded towards me,
They crash - I'm floating, down, down, down.

Flora MacPhail (11)
Leighton Middle School

FIRE

Fire can be cool,
Though not if you're a fool,
Fire is hot,
It can make things rot.

Dancing, flickering flames,
Reflecting on the windowpanes,
Orange, yellow and red,
Make sure the flames don't catch your head!

Fire goes out in the rain,
Which can sometimes be a pain,
Orange, yellow and red,
Make sure the flames don't catch your head!

Fire can be cool,
Though not if you're a fool,
Fire is hot,
It can make things *rot!*

Dawn Mayne (11)
Leighton Middle School

HUNTER

Fins cut through glassy water,
Black waves, obsidian dark.
Scars from forgotten fights,
Eyes as silent as the night.

A forgotten warrior,
Slow curves through deep dark water, diving slowly,
Sharp, hard eyes, deadly,
Hunter of the silence, ghostly.

Sudden fin-flashes -
Swift flick of a tail.
Water billows red.
Dives again.

Fins cut through glassy water,
Black waves, obsidian dark.
The sad, dark eyes of the hunter,
The sad, dark eyes of the shark.

Lauren Stone (11)
Leighton Middle School

The Wall

The wall is bored and no one cares,
It's almost as if: it's not there.
Bored it sits, almost forever,
People make it loose its tether!

A fly crawls up through the door,
Telling wall about the floor.
For wall cannot see much more,
Than the table and the door.

Who invented our friend wall?
Maybe no one did at all,
Perhaps instinct, evolving fast.
Where would we be, in the past?
Try help people, let it be.
Let them see without the wall to make our house,
Where on earth would we be?
Dead?

Camilla Barbosa-Jefferson (11)
Leighton Middle School

Aquarius

A quarius has always been the loyal face in the crowd
Q ueens admire his honesty
U nlike some he is the one to rely on
A nd he views life through original eyes as the world flows by
R ushing is not his style, he's not slow either, but he'll make a mile
I n the dark night sky he shines out stronger than the rest
U nlike some he shall never lie
S trong, as he is the water-carrier with weights of 1 ton steel.

Thomas Wood (11)
Linslade Middle School

ENGLAND VS GERMANY

In the first few minutes of the football match,
It started when the German keeper made a good catch,
Germany broke across from Nole,
Yanker passed it in the goal,
Oh no, what's happened? The Germans are ahead,
England are playing like they're still in bed,
8 minutes later, Owen puts it to a draw,
The German crowd started to snore,
Then Gerrard's foot and the ball met,
When Gerrard cracked it in the net,
Owen got England another,
Neville looked happy, he's Gary's brother,
The final whistle blew, hooray, hooray,
A great victory for England today!

Kevin Edwards (12)
Linslade Middle School

MY LIFE

Up high away in my little brain of mine,
Closing my eyes tightly, visioning stars shining brightly,
I was born in a warm, comfortable and see-through bed,
With stars shining brightly above my head.
From that very moment my life was secretly full of fun.
Right up till I could speak, my toddler life had gone as
Quick as a tick and before I knew it, I was a grown lady
With problems growing around my head.
Now I'm nearly a teenager with fashion building up around my skin,
I just hope this life lasts longer than my others, which lasted a tick.

Elise Thomas (10)
Linslade Middle School

How Could You?

I have sparkled here for a million years
Watching the Earth turn round and round
Watched people be happy, sad and shedding tears
I have seen leaves fall to the ground

I have seen happiness and devastation
I wonder how that could happen
I'm amazed by how you use respiration
Also how you can kill an innocent lapin

You have come so far but still
You kill and try to kill your planet
You think yourself brill
You can't leave anything alone, not even granite

Still you cannot touch me
As I watch you kill yourselves
There is still time
Even as you blow up yourselves
I'll still be.
Some of you live in stars
Some live in grime.

Jo Bailey-Watson (11)
Linslade Middle School

The Beach

The sun shining on the sand,
I can hear someone playing in a band,
The stones and shells,
The donkeys' bells,
I love to lie on the beach.

The beautiful gleaming sun,
The children are having fun,
The seagulls flying by,
A kite is flying high,
I love to lie on the beach.

Sophie Hing (11)
Linslade Middle School

THE STARS

I wonder about those stars up there,
Making shapes in the sky,
How fortune-tellers tell the future,
And amaze us by predicting.

I'm a Capricorn, always patient, organising my busy life,
Full of ambition trying to complete dreams,
Always doing work that has to be done.

The universe is so big, I wonder how far it goes?
The stars show the way for those lost at night,
Three wise men follow a star to their king.

There must be more than nine planets,
I'd love to go to space,
To see the universe and make a poem that rolls everything into one,
To catch the spirits of everybody.

The sky is unpredictable, even to us,
It can change at a click of a finger,
Sunshine to rain and back, we can never be prepared,
That's why it's good to have stars to light up the way.

Richard Savill (11)
Linslade Middle School

ARIES

My life was born under the stars
My name is Aries
My wool on my back is hairy
So I'll knot you my life

They say that I'm confident
I'll guide you to a special place
I'll put you through your paces
A life behind the stars

The quick ram they say
I'll show my stars tonight
As I fly through the night
I'll guide you through your days

Fun, oh yes fun
My life is like a game

Because Aries is my name!

Helen Humphreys (11)
Linslade Middle School

CAPRICORN

Good with money
Sweet as honey
Moody in the head
Love my bed

Dreaming sweetly
So day-dreamy
Big birthday bash
Love swimming and making a splash!

Animals lovely
Rather cuddly
Chocolate sweet
I have small feet

Sometimes bad
Hardly ever sad
Celebrate with gratitude
Especially when I receive new shoes.

Natashia McKenzie-Cook (11)
Linslade Middle School

STARS

Stars glistening in the stars at night
They glow brightly
In the pitch-black sky at night.

Some of them mean different signs
Capricorn, Virgo, Sagittarius, Libra,
They all have different meanings.

There are lots more too,
Leo, Scorpio, Taurus, Aries,
Faithful, passionate, placid, confident.

Gemini, Cancer, Pisces, Aquarius,
They all mean different things,
Youthful, shrewd, sensitive, honest.

Star signs are made by the Greeks,
People still use them today
To see what future they seek.

Lisa Baczynski (11)
Linslade Middle School

ZODIAC SIGNS

The zodiac sign
Pisces the kind thoughtful fish
And peaceful in mind

The zodiac sign
Kind, loyal Aquarius
Water-carrier

The zodiac sign
Aries, the quick fun-filled ram
Confident and smart

The zodiac sign
Taurus, the smart bull
Placid and patient

The zodiac sign
Always loving and faithful
Leo the lion.

Kerry Mittins (11)
Linslade Middle School

CANCER

I am cancer, brave and strong
I am intelligent and I'll live long
I am protective and have my head held high
I am a man and I'll do nothing with a sigh.

Ben East (11)
Linslade Middle School

SCORPIO

Scorpio, oh Scorpio, why do you sting?
You don't know how much it hurts,
But still I love the way your tail curls round,
You force me into anything, and that is what I hate.

Scorpio, tell me, don't you like being passionate?
You only like to sting enemies,
But if you sting your enemies, that means you don't like me!

Well, what can I say? How can this be?
You have hurt my friends,
They are poisoned and might not live,
What can I have done to you?

Hayleigh McDonald (11)
Linslade Middle School

PINCHER

The seeking crab is very shrewd,
He is not at all a little bit rude.
Up he is at the top of space,
Not falling down because he's on a strawberry lace.

One day he'll rule all of Heaven,
Maybe up above on top of Devon.
The crab twinkles because he's protective,
So he'll save the world because he's a detective.

Philip Trott (11)
Linslade Middle School

FEELINGS

I'm on top of the world
I'm feeling really happy
And it's you that makes me happy
Thank you stars
Thank you stars

But other days I feel sad
I feel really down
And it's you that makes me sad
Thank you stars
Thank you stars

And some days I feel nice
It's only happened twice
And it's you that makes me nice
Thank you stars
Thank you stars

Other days I feel bad
I feel really naughty
And it's you that makes me bad
Thank you stars
Thank you stars

Sometimes I feel angry
I feel really mad
And it's you that makes me mad
Thank you stars
Thank you stars.

Samantha Cundell (11)
Linslade Middle School

DAVID BLAINE

David Blaine
He'll never hide
Always taking
A short stride.

Biting your given
Quarter in half
He'll make you scream
He'll make you laugh.

Don't forget
He'll levitate
You'll run away
And be gobsmacked mate.

Do you remember
When he froze himself?
It was not magic
It was a matter of health.

Frozen for
A long weekend
Inside he thought
It would never end.

You better be careful
What you think
He can mind-read
And make you drink!

Kieran Billington
Linslade Middle School

Cancer Stars

The crab so strong, so sharp,
He rides the water like a fast carp.

He is protective, all to win his love,
To guard his stars up above.

He's up in the sky, looking in space,
To come and fight and win his race.

His hands so strong like sharp claws,
With golden pearls in his paws.

His enemies dark, his allies light,
He'd never go down without a fight.

He is Cancer, the zodiac ever,
He protects his love, to kill, he would never!

Christopher George (11)
Linslade Middle School

Zodiac

Twinkling stars in the cool summer's night
Lying on their little beds shining bright
They give us light

Near twinkling stars
Is a planet called Mars
But space is sadly behind bars.

Emma Harfield (11)
Linslade Middle School

HOROSCOPE

I don't think that they are true
The things they write about me or you
They tell the things that are going to happen
And if you look carefully they go in a pattern
They tell your future for the week
And all the good things you are going to seek
They call it a horoscope
And what they write I do hope
How can they tell
What's going to happen to me
And my friend Mel?
What are your reactions when they say
You are going to meet the man of your dreams today?
I really do hope some day they come true
And I hope for you too
I will carry all my dreams
When I go sailing down the stream.

Laura Keable (12)
Linslade Middle School

ZODIAC

Looking down on the Earth down there,
A child is born on a certain star,
Riding along through the crystal sky,
Shouting and cheering, thinking he can fly.

Laura Taylor (11)
Linslade Middle School

WINTER

As I go round,
With my coat wrapped round me
And the grass turns white and the ponds all freeze,
The earth dies underneath my feet.

I frighten all birds away,
The plants all disappear
And long before the warmth of spring
Animals retreat from my coldness.

My frosty, bitter cruelness
Is enough to scare the daylights
Out of everyone and everything
Who belongs to this universe.

I have no mercy on any weedy
Flora or fauna that
Are idiotic enough
To lie in my path of flight.

I silence the singing of birds,
I please man with Christmas
And crispy, crunchy, chilly
Chalk-white snow.

Long nights, short days,
Bitter, raw, perishing, bleak,
Cheery, festive, spirited,
Are all part of my extraordinary package.

Anna Head (11)
Linslade Middle School

FRIENDSHIP

You and I shall always have friendship
No matter what may part us
Being close or far away
Even if your name is Gus
We will be friends forever
And during all kinds of weather
Always,
Always
And
Always
Together.

I meant what I said
I said what I meant
A best friend is forever
One hundred per cent.

Caylin Joski-Jethi (11)
Linslade Middle School

ZODIAC

The stars shine bright on a winter's night,
The icicles freeze in a cold icy breeze,
The snow falls gently on the old brick wall,
The old man sleeps in his soft warm sheets.

The birds have sung, morning has come,
The air is crisp and polluted with mist,
The old man wakes and pours tea in his cup,
The sky is blue, the sun is through.

James Bishop (11)
Linslade Middle School

STARS

Stars depend on who you are
They shine up bright from afar.
Stars live up in the sky
Shooting ones go whizzing by.

Horoscopes are made by stars
Are you like the god called Mars?
People could be joyful or happy
Or they could be sad and snappy.

Do you know what star you are?
It could cause you to buy a flash car.
If you see a star in the sky
Just don't walk by!

Helen Yates (11)
Linslade Middle School

UNICORN

As the unicorn jumps through the air
the wind catches his shimmering hair.
His horn of ivory, his hooves of gold,
he gallops through the winter's cold.
He gallops through the forest fast,
he's found his place of rest at last.
He settles down right by a tree,
at last, from capture, he is free.

Andrew Reeves (11)
Linslade Middle School

THE ZODIACS

The bull, Taurus, is my star sign
And my childhood life is going just fine
My best friend is Aries
Our little star shines from afar
My dad is Gemini
His tiny star is in the endless sky
Now what's my mum? Err,
Oh yeah, Cancer,
Up in the sky, I wish I could fly,
For then I could hold my little star,
It would have a little smile
And people would go, arrr!

Avril Dowdeswell (11)
Linslade Middle School

SPACE CRYSTALS

Crystals sparkle in the light,
But I can't understand why they're rare,
Because when I look into the night,
I see crystals shining there.

Emily Sheppard (11)
Linslade Middle School

ZODIAC DREAMER

I'm telling this story,
Of ultimate glory
In case you travel to a mystic land
And as it is you
I say this quite true
I believe this story is quite grand!

Now, Pisces is a mysterious soul
For he hovers all day under water
It makes one think what he does all the time
Just swim through coral all covered in grime

Poor Aries on those cold misty hills
Calls and brays for a friend
Does he wonder all day where to turn, which way
Thinking, 'Well, where does it end?'

There's Scorpio running on hot desert sands
Cowering under rocks for shade
He's under the rules of the sun
There's nowhere to run

Taurus, the wise friendly bull
Is always there for a friend in need
He's truly great, completely true
Taurus stops you from feeling blue.

But what about the other eight
Just sit and think in curiosity
A zodiac depends on who you are
They shine so brightly from afar.

Laura Driscoll (11)
Linslade Middle School

Mourning Star

A solitary shooting star,
Eternally burns across the sky,
A lonely ball of flame to burn,
In the reflection of my mind's eye.
I watch my bright illumination,
As it begins its soft descent,
Leaving me with nothing, but
A painful, burning, dark lament.

Somewhere in my sanctuary,
Graceful footsteps tread once more,
These memories of future dreams
And memories themselves foresworn.
Sands of time slip through my fingers,
Although I beg for them to stay,
My pleas fall on deaf ears of ghosts,
Incense wishes fly away.

Why did those times have to die?
Am I destined to bear these eternal scars?
Will I ever spread my wings and fly? Am I just another mourning star?
From this place those times have fled,
With memories never to be found,
Childhood's magical dreams and hopes,
Remorselessly burned to the ground.

Yet, glowing in the darkness,
Somewhere, a heart not to be tamed
And from the embers of crushed velvet,
My Phoenix rises from the flames
And even now in this eternal dark,
A shooting star still shines through,
Because when you wish upon a star,
Incense wishes can still come true.

Steven Parker (16)
Luton Sixth Form College

THE COUNTRYSIDE TRAIN

There is the smoke
There is the steam
Here comes the iron horse
Fulfilled with dreams
People are sad
People are happy
Let's turn around
And make it snappy
There are the people standing by
There is a baby as quiet as the night
There is the smoke
There is the steam
Some of the people are not very clean
Horses and cattle
Hill and plain
Goodbye everybody
We're leaving again.

Claire Gazeley (16)
Luton Sixth Form College

THE TWIN TOWERS

I was driving down the road when crumbles
One of the Twin Towers, I hear screams
I hear mumbles
The poor souls trapped inside
Some now jumping into the now black skies
As the glass and debris tumbles
Another plane flying low, hits
The second with an almighty
Blow!

Lee Turner (12)
Marston Vale Middle School

RANCID

In the jungle of integrityless tripe
Stand four tattooed explorers
Venturing out into the past
Their Mohicans and spikes
Padded jackets and cargo shorts
Boots and shaven heads
Bleached jeans and braces
Studded leather jackets and padlocks
Signify they are the last of their ilk
Once they've gone
The jungle will again be deserted of the truth
And the class of 1977 will die
These are the last of the hardcore punks.

Miles Sloan (12)
Marston Vale Middle School

FRIENDS

Friends can be fun
Friends can be caring
Friends can be sharing
Friends can be told secrets that won't tell
Friends can be trustworthy
Friends support one another
Friends don't backstab
Friends tell friends everything if they're upset
Friends will listen and sort things out
Friends don't take boys away.

Lauren Smith (12)
Marston Vale Middle School

A Soldier's Lament

Emotions course though
My veins, like lightning striking,
Fear, excitement - love.

To the war I go,
One of untold millions, I
March towards my fate.

On the battlefield,
I kill to protect my home,
While comrades lie dead.

Generals wait behind
The lines, from dead and wounded
They heed not a cry.

After conflict, youth
Lies torn, fading fast, like a
Half-remembered dream.

Will Mason-Wilkes (12)
Marston Vale Middle School

Friends

Friends can be fun
Friends are always there for you
You can talk to them about girlie stuff
Friends can be trustworthy
And you can go shopping with them
And they won't tell a soul.

Tessa-Louise Tringham (12)
Marston Vale Middle School

Unicorn

Mummy, there's a horse at the stables
A dreamy, beautiful mare
Yet she seems so strange and mystic
With her tranquil pure white hair

Mummy, there's a horse at the stables
Who's not always there
And although she's strong and silent
She always seems to care

Mummy, there's a horse at the stables
Who likes to do and dare
But is that a horn's tip
Disappearing into thin air . . .

Fern Blevins (11)
Marston Vale Middle School

In The World

Every day I am sat at home
Thinking about the world
One day I will be out there alone
Scared, not knowing what to do
Just sitting there with nothing to do
One day I will be stuck at home
But some families aren't all together
They are somewhere in the world
Thinking about my life and one day
I won't be alone.

Louise Moynham (12)
Marston Vale Middle School

THE TUMBLING TWIN TOWERS

The 11th of September, a day of devastation,
It was going to be a day of annihilation.

When the aeroplanes hit, the people would shout,
'Help me God, help me get out.'

There were helpless people trapped inside
And hundreds of people had already died.

Lots of parents picked up the phone
And said to their children, 'I'm not coming home.'

The blazing fire was too much for a man,
But they said to themselves, 'I'll do what I can.'

The people had to make two choices and then they frowned,
It was either die from the fire, or die from hitting the ground.

There were people screaming, shouting and even crying,
There were wounded people, hurt and dying.

People thought to themselves, 'Is there really God or Jesus?
Because if there is, then why don't they free us?'

Christopher Woodward (13)
Marston Vale Middle School

CHOCOLATE...

Is the most glorious thing.
Mars bar, Twix, Bounty.
It tastes like Heaven, soft and creamy.
Galaxy, Milky Way.

A Snowflake by Cadbury's
Is simply the best,
With crumbly white flakes
Covered in milk chocolate.

Cadbury's Aero is supreme,
The way the bubbly
Chocolate melts in your mouth,
It makes you feel relaxed.

Heather Welsh (11)
Marston Vale Middle School

IT DOESN'T MATTER

My teddy has one eye
and only one ear,
but that doesn't matter

My book has no cover
and is losing three pages,
but that doesn't matter

My ball has no spots
and nobody to play with,
but that doesn't matter

My dog has three legs
and only one ear,
but that doesn't matter

My clock has four numbers
and only one hand,
but that doesn't matter

My rabbit has no ears
and no tail,
but that doesn't matter

All of these things are not perfect,
but that doesn't matter.

Daniel Spiers (12)
Marston Vale Middle School

I Wish...

I wish I had a hippo
Big, fat and strong
I wish I had a hippo
For all day long
I wish I had a hippo
With grey, wrinkly skin
I wish I had a hippo
But it would make an awful din!

I wish I had a monkey
Swinging through the trees
I wish I had a monkey
To be friends with me
I wish I had a monkey
Chatting all day long
I wish I had a monkey
But it would let off an awful pong!

I wish I had no brother
To tease me all day
I wish I had no brother
It's just the things he says
I wish I had no brother
To play the violin
I wish I had no brother
It really is a sin!

Nicola Coop (11)
Marston Vale Middle School

FRIDAYS AND WEEKENDS

Hooray! Hooray!
It's Friday today,
School's out,
Let's scream and shout.
Time to party,
Time to play,
The weekend's coming on its way,
Although I wish it will stay.
Saturday morning swimming is fun,
Dinner time,
How I enjoy burger in a bun.
It's afternoon,
Time to clean my room,
Oh what a drag,
Grrrrr . . .
Saturday night,
It's curry night,
Stay up late,
Films are great.
Sunday morning,
Lay in till late,
Get up and play with my mate,
I come in late,
Roast chicken on my plate.
Early to bed,
Monday morning I dread.

Natasha Freeman (11)
Marston Vale Middle School

I Once Rode A Horse Called . . .

I once rode a horse called Kitty
whose face was filled with pity
along came a man
with a dark brown tan
and said, 'Oh isn't she pretty.'

I once rode a horse called Annie
whose back was small and crammy
a boy came that day
and rode all that way
to London with his brother, Danny.

I once rode a horse called Sparkle
who you could easily startle
he once bucked me off
and ran away with a cough
leaving me sitting in a pile of charcoal.

Debbie Fisher (11)
Marston Vale Middle School

In The Garden

In the garden birds are singing and chirping,
Butterflies flutter in the sky,
Fish are swimming in the pond,
The day has just begun,
The sun is out, what a wonderful day!
You can hear the children play, running, screaming
And shouting out loud,
It's night-time already,
There's not a sound to be heard and nothing to be seen.

Karissa France (12)
Marston Vale Middle School

THE LOST SPIRITS

The lost spirits calling
As the day is dawning . . .
They're drifting in the house that's
Full of spooks and frights . . .
And no one will go there on cold
Winter midnights . . .

Except the boy that knew nothing of
These spooks and frights,
On cold winter midnights.

As he heard a creak,
He feared even to speak,
He did not know what was going on
And before he knew it, he was
Gone!

Richard Collins (11)
Marston Vale Middle School

MY CAT!

I have a girl cat called Felix
When she has a mad turn she runs
Up and down the stairs
She sleeps at the end of my bed
On her blanket
She likes to have a fuss
With anyone
She doesn't like my rabbits
But at night-time she likes
To snuggle up with me
Nice and tight.

Hannah Bennett-Cook (12)
Marston Vale Middle School

WHAT AM I?

A lung full of fire,
A breath full of steam,
A back full of spikes,
A nose full of flames,

Skin tough as leather,
Skin rough as rock,
Skin purple as purple can be,
Skin hot as fire,

Teeth as sharp as a sword,
Teeth as dirty as mud,
Teeth in rows of about 20,
Teeth also very big,

A lung full of fire,
A lung full of steam,
A throat full of ashes,
A nose not very clean,

A height as high as a tower,
A height that is very scary,
A height that is above them all,
A height that can see everything,

A wing made for flying,
A wing very thin,
A wing orange and purple,
A wing that can blow away steam.

What am I?

A dragon.

Tristan Moore (12)
Marston Vale Middle School

Untitled

Naughty boys get into trouble
They are really bad
If they upset someone I knew
I'd be really sad

They think that they are big and hard
And that they rule the school
They wear shades and jackets
And think that they are cool

They whistle at the girls
And the girls whistle back
Bruce is the big one
His bag is a potato sack

Once he was running in sports day
And running against me
Someone had to win
But who would it be?

Bruce was running faster
And faster without a sound
But in a flash he tripped
And fell to the ground

I finished the race in first place
I was smiling at my win
I got a trophy
Bruce got a tin

Bruce is now a good boy
And well contented too
He helps me when I get stuck
On a sum like 9+2.

David Pugh (12)
Marston Vale Middle School

THE MAN WHO INVENTED CRICKET

The man who invented cricket,
must have been dead clever.
He didn't have all of the whites
or any clothes whatever!

The man who invented cricket,
he hadn't even a ball,
or pads, but only his hairy legs
and biscons head that's all!

The man who invented cricket,
for him, he said where at,
but if you hit it too high,
he thought the catch and 'Howzat'.

The cave wall as the boundary,
the wind was the referee,
when the man who did it, did it,
in 30,000 BC!

Ben Eagles (12)
Marston Vale Middle School

UP ON CLOUD NUMBER NINE

On cloud number nine,
It is a lovely sight from up here
And it feels fine,
You can see miles away from here.

The wind blows in your face
And the clouds move side to side,
Up on cloud nine is a fabulous place,
There are lots of places to hide.

The angels go flying past,
They send messages to people,
They never go very fast,
Now I have to go back to Stepel Lane.

Lydia Freeman (12)
Marston Vale Middle School

THE MOON

In the night it shines brightly
With that glamour glow,
It lies in-between the stars
You can watch it from below.

The sun gives off its light
So this planet shines brightly too,
It's like a pretty painting
Painted especially for you.

If you don't know what it is
But, I'm sure you must have guessed,
Yes, it's the moon
And by far the very best.

You see the moon is very special
In almost every way,
It's been like this forever
And forever it shall stay.

Kerri Shorter (11)
Marston Vale Middle School

THE CASTLE OF WAR

The castle stood dilapidated and cold against the miserable
background that was war.
The shrill sound of guns blasting through its fortresses.
The haunting wail of death filled the castle with anger.

As a fierce wind blew, another ten men were gone.
'Go!' shouted the sergeant. Fearful men charged up the winding
staircase to the top of the tower.
As the enemy awaited their arrival at the top, the fifteen men headed to
certain death.

As the first man appeared, on the ground below him,
the enemy fired.
The castle of war howled in pain, its crumbling bricks falling like rain
on an April's day.
But the castle was saddened further; as in its foundations lay the soon
rotting corpses of fifteen men forced to die.

Victoria Taylor (11)
Marston Vale Middle School

NATURE

Nature is as beautiful as a baby being born,
Nature is as beautiful as the sun setting in the evening,
Nature is as beautiful as a baby bird hatching.

Nature is as beautiful as a heart-warming picture,
Nature is as beautiful as peace in the world,
Nature is as beautiful as you and me.

Mica Smith (12)
Marston Vale Middle School

SNAKES AND LADDERS

S mooth, slimy snakes
N aughty, nifty things
A lways hunting everywhere, he always finds someone
K ing of the board
E ating all the counters, going back to one
S adly saying goodbye to every other one

A dding to this story
N ever read again
D ice are all we need to play the game

L adders, long as well
A lthough they're nice, they are there to help you win the game
D o you know how to play?
D addy told me they also bring good luck
E xciting and fun it is
R eady to play the game of
S nakes and ladders!

Samantha Grummitt (11)
Marston Vale Middle School

I HATE

I hate the way you make me smile,
I hate the way you lie,
I hate the way you make me cry,
I hate the way you talk,
I hate the way you make me feel,
I hate the way you walk,
I hate the way you make me laugh,
I hate the way you run away,
I hate the way you left me here,
I hate the way you're not coming back.

Kayleigh Pratt (12)
Marston Vale Middle School

My Dog

I have a dog called Oliver
he loves lots of cuddles
his nose is wet
and enjoys lots of snuggles

He's friendly as a friendly thing
nothing's as cute as him
he smells like rosemary
and likes to howl and sing

His ears are long
his nose is short
and has very ploddy paws
when he's asleep he really snores

I have a dog called Oliver
he loves lots of cuddles
his nose is wet
and enjoys lots of snuggles.

I luv him.

Eleanor Jay (11)
Marston Vale Middle School

Teachers' Wishes

Teachers wish for pupils to be
Witty, brave and smart
Even in good and bad subjects
Like English, maths or art.

Teachers wish for us to be
Good, polite and kind
To never swear at all
And to always have a good mind.

Teachers' wishes are always about school
Teachers' wishes are not very cruel
Teachers' wishes are not really cool
But pupils wish there was no school.

Laura Jeffery (12)
Marston Vale Middle School

NIGHT-TIME THOUGHTS

Horses are so wonderful,
Horses are much fun,
Every time I fall off,
I always hurt my . . .

Racing across the fields,
At ninety miles per hour,
Passing the other riders,
Makes them really sour.

The men look attractive,
Dressed in their red suits,
The hunting horn then blows
And we follow in pursuit.

Jumping over hedges,
Splashing through the brooks,
Oh this is the life,
Walking will not do.

Hurry, hurry, hurry,
We're racing for the cup,
It's really getting exciting now,
Oh no, I've just woken up.

Jade Goff (11)
Marston Vale Middle School

IN THE PARK

Sitting around
Like a lonely cloud
I wait for my friends.

The swings are blowing in the wind,
The roundabout is not spinning around,
And I, sitting alone on the bench.

Then I hear laughs and screams from the road, it's them, my friends.

We play on the swings 'til dark.

We all go home our separate ways until tomorrow at school.

But what if they didn't show? I would be left on my own in the dark,
Until my mum had told me to go home.

What would you do?

Lucy Hourihan (11)
Marston Vale Middle School

WHAT DO YOU SEE IN ME?

Have you ever seen the sky as blue as the sea?
What do you see in me?
Have you ever seen my house as tall as a flat?
What do you see in me?

Have you ever seen my room so bright?
What do you see in me?
You look on the bed, I'm fast asleep,
Now what do you see in me?

Melanie Dunne (12)
Marston Vale Middle School

I Wish I Had An Elephant

I wish I had an elephant
to carry me everywhere.
I wish I had an elephant
with green and purple hair.
I wish I had an elephant
that would always care.
I wish I had an elephant
to be there when I'm sad.
I wish I had an elephant
who loved me when I'm bad.

I wish I had an elephant
that didn't grow too big.
But if he grew and grew
he'd have to live in the zoo,
And I'd get a hippo instead!

Amy Mould (11)
Marston Vale Middle School

A Springer Spaniel

Springer spaniel,
they're springy spaniels,
they are great fun,
they love to run,
they catch things and drop things
and their ears fall in their water bowl,
but they love getting wet,
they're soppy and sweet,
they love their cuddles,
but that's a springer spaniel.

Emily-Jane Wilson (11)
Marston Vale Middle School

THE BEST POEM EVER!

C alm as a baby sleeping,
A ble as an artist,
N atural like a tree,
C reative like my dad,
E asy going when people are stressed,
R ough like a lion

A lways alert when something goes wrong,
B etter than anyone else,
I maginative, I don't think so!
G etting there on time sometimes,
A bigail is a wicked name,
I t's the best poem ever,
L oving every minute of it!

Abigail Horton (11)
Mill Vale Middle School

LEO, LEO, LEO

L over of attention like Robbie Williams,
E xtroverted like a best friend to everybody,
O rganised as a dog digging a hole for its home.

T echnical like a professor working on a robot,
H orrendous like a funny clown,
O ptimistic like an explorer getting lost,
M ysterious like a detective on a mission
A lways takes part in anything like a bird coming to a big crowd
S ometimes gets annoyed with sister, like a cat and a dog.

Thomas Peirce (11)
Mill Vale Middle School

GEMINI, JO

G ifted like a generous Gemini,
E njoy being sociable like a party animal,
M entally ambitious like an eager explorer,
I ngenious like a practicing professor,
N imble like a leggy lizard,
I maginative like an ambitious author

J oke: I don't think I'm nimble,
O utside in my own time is more me,
A lways helping like a good Samaritan,
N ever naughty - well, only at home,
N ever would I miss the chance to cook, never,
A nd I'm always around for other people.

Joanna Solley (11)
Mill Vale Middle School

WHO I AM

A mibitious like a determined child.
R esourceful as an original musician.
I nnovative like England's Prime Minister.
E nthusiastic as an eager girl ready to go.
S elf assured like a protective cat.

M entally active as a jack-in-the-box.
I ndividual with my own mind.
C oncerned like a worry wart.
H elpful as an angel from Heaven.
A cting hard to reach my goal.
E legant like a tip-toeing fairy.
L oving animals, big or small.
A mazing, never knowing what I will say next.

Michaela Penny (11)
Mill Vale Middle School

THAT'S ME

T alented like an actress singing and dancing.
A chieving certificates like a student graduating.
U nderstanding like an adult - sorting out problems.
R elaxed like teachers in the staff room.
U nlucky like never winning the lottery.
S tubborn, always thinking about myself.

D anielle, a nice person? . . . Well, I think so.
A n unlucky person - I think so.
N ever relaxed - always up and about.
I nvestigator like the FBI
E nergetic like an athlete - well thank you.
L ively like a partier - I love parties.
L oving all the boys - ha ha.
E xciting, always up for things.

Danielle McGrath (11)
Mill Vale Middle School

AQUARIUS, MY STAR SIGN

A ltruistic like a charity worker
Q uick like a cheetah
U npredictable like a tornado
A rtful like a bank manager
R espective like a priest
I nventive like an artist
U nique like a butterfly
S cientific like a scientist

A rgumentative like a dog with a bone
D etermined like a bird on a journey
A rtistic like a painter
M essy like my bedroom.

Adam Regan (11)
Mill Vale Middle School

LEO, LAURA

L eader like a lion born to lead!
E xtroverted like a charity worker
O ptimistic like a game show contestant

L imelight lover - totally true
A mbitious - I think so
U nconfident - never
R arely loud - I think that's true
A lso an organiser - in my dreams

C ompetitive? Can be
O pen and comforting - would be
L ots of dignified decisions - better than none
L ittle charisma - true, true
I 'm honourable - in a billion years
N ot dramatic - as if
S unny - that's me.

Laura Collins (11)
Mill Vale Middle School

VIRGO

V ery good, like an angel
I nto computer games like a computer freak
R eady like an organiser
G ets confused all the time
O bstanant when doing some things

I nto computer games, of course!
A lways confused, sometimes
N ever organised, well sometimes.

Ian Sharp (12)
Mill Vale Middle School

PISCES

P sychic like a well-paid fortune teller
I maginative like a little child
S erious like an angry teacher
C reative like a famous artist
E motional like a little baby
S hy like a little orphan

B eing psychic – I wish I was!
E motional as I am, sometimes when I don't expect it.
T hinking creatively all the time.
H iding and being shy is me in new company.
A nyone can get serious but not for long or like me.
N one of these are just like me ... except ...
Y es? Thinking creatively.

Bethany Hilton (11)
Mill Vale Middle School

I AM ...

P eace-loving like a good god in the sky,
I mpressionable like Robin Williams in a cartoon,
S piritual like a haunting ghost,
C reative like Leonardo da Vinci ready to paint,
E ven forthright like a team leader ready to shout,
S erious like a court judge ready to pass sentence.

L ively like an energetic toddler ready to play,
A dreamer who dreams a big future ahead,
U sually alone and called a psychic,
R eally imaginative like an editor,
E very day flit away as also shyness,
N ever worried about the next step in life.

Lauren May Mackenzie (11)
Mill Vale Middle School

Everything You Need To Know About Me

P eace-loving like a lion taking care of its baby
I maginative is like a poem
S uper sensitive is like a lonely little flower
C haritable like a big charity
E ffective is like when you make something happen
S hy is like a long dark tree

C aring like a concerned nurse
H armless like a piece of grass
A nxious like the white rabbit
R esponsible like a doctor
L ikeable like a best friend
O rganised like a queen
T errified like a soldier going into battle
T rustful like a judge
E nergetic like wanting to do sports and exercises.

Charlotte Smith (11)
Mill Vale Middle School

All About Me

V ery practical like a sneaky snake
I ntelligent as a book
R esponsible as a caring mother
G etting somewhere on time
O ver convinced as a hungry lion

C areful planner! Am I?
L ogical - me? Of course.
A ll important as a judge
I ntroverted as a shy rabbit
R omatic - that's me!
E ager to learn things? Me - sometimes.

Claire Parker (12)
Mill Vale Middle School

AQUARIUS STAR SIGN

A ltruistic as a relief worker handing out papers
Q ualified like a school teacher
U nique like a robot
A lone as a detached house
R easoning like a judge at court
I ngenious like an inventor at work
U nconventional like a family with brown hair with red tones
S cientific like a scientist

S cientific, sorry that's not me
T icklish to the touch
U nusual, you've come to the right person
A lways trying my best
R eliable, that's me
T errific, I'm your boy.

Stuart Lee Nash (11)
Mill Vale Middle School

MY FAMILY

C alm like my goldfish
A rgumentative like my sister
N obody can be as moody as me
C onscientious like my hard-working dad
E motional like my mum watching a sad film
R eserved like my hamster

D emanding like my moany dad
A ngry like my mad dog
V iolent like my mum's hand
I maginative like my sister with her art work
D ramatic like my dog.

David Isaac (11)
Mill Vale Middle School

My Mystic Star Sign And Name

S trong-willed
A lways loves to go out
G regarious as a person out with his mates
I dealistic like an impractical person
T ravels like an excited traveller
T ranquil as a calm puddle
A brupt like a sudden movement
R estless as an impatient person
I s always honest
U ncertain as an afraid person or animal
S tudious as an eager pupil

M oody? – As if!
A lways loves to go out – I always do!
R estless – most of the time
T ranquil – yeah, right!
Y eah! I reckon I'm strong-willed!
N ever be an impractical person!

Martyn Tallon (11)
Mill Vale Middle School

All About Me

L onely - sometimes but hardly ever
E ntertaining - that's me *ha ha* joke
A rtistic - well that's what my teachers say to me
N ice to others especially my friends
N ever bad because I like to help people a lot
E nter my life and see what it's like.

Leanne Frimley (12)
Mill Vale Middle School

IT'S ALL ABOUT ME

A ssertive like a policeman on the beat,
R evengeful like a teacher with a grudge,
I nnovative like a new manager with new ideas,
E nthusiastic like a football player,
S elf assured like an actor.

L ewis, assertive never!
E nthusiastic maybe?
W anted to be a boss someday,
I like getting revenge on people
S elf indulgent maybe but not self assured.

Lewis Collins (11)
Mill Vale Middle School

ALL ABOUT ME

L oving like a lion to its cub
I dealistic like a teacher to a child
B rave like a bungee jumper being pushed off the side
R esponsible like a parent to its children
A ffable like a very good friend.

Elizabeth Sansom (12)
Mill Vale Middle School

VIRGO

V icious like a lion hunting its prey.
I nward looking like a mouse.
R esponsible like a group of police officers.
G etting there on time like a paramedic.
O rganised like a lawyer in a courtroom.

Elliott Jaggs (11)
Mill Vale Middle School

LEO

L ikes the limelight like a star in a movie
E xtroverted, loves company like a friendly person
O rganiser, someone who likes things like my mum

R esponsibility, to be in charge of something
O bject, to say you are not in favour
S unny, a very cheerful person
I rritating, very annoying just like my sister
E xtraordinary, a very unusual person like my dad who loves off-roading

K eep caring like a nurse
I maginative like a fortune teller
R ich as the queen of hearts
B rainy like a scientist
Y ards full of horses.

Rosie Kirby (11)
Mill Vale Middle School

THE CHASE

Walking home from my friend's one night
A man jumped out and gave me a fright
I started to run
When I looked back he was chasing me
Tripped over
I banged my head
When I got up
I couldn't see
I finally made it round the corner
Phew, he let me be.

Aisha Brown (13)
Northfields Upper School

WHAT A CAT!

You're so dark, there's no light,
When a dog barks, it gives you a fright.
You leap the wall, where you look very tall.
Then you leap over to the other side,
Luckily you've got nine lives.
Your senses tell you where to go,
You always know where's the flow.
There you go, through the flap
Looking like a little rat.
There you smell something delicious,
There you turn very vicious.
There you run, fast as a lion,
Making your paws turn to fire.
Finally you're there, eating your food,
Ummm, that's good.
After that, you leap on my lap,
Purring away, feeling safe.
Then you fall straight to sleep,
Fur all woolly like a sheep.
There I put you on the warm mat,
Oh God, 'What a cat'.

Lucy Partridge (13)
Northfields Upper School

LA PROMENADE. LA FEMME A L'OMBRELLE

She turned away from me,
Her face shrouded in mist
And cast her shadow over me.
Despite the sun and fair weather
Doubt froze me, saying never.

But the sun and field scream
'All is possible if you can dream!'
Dreams are lies and nothing more
All they do is open the door,
So you can fall through to despair.

Brenden Delaney (15)
Northfields Upper School

GIRLS

Girls this year,
always interfere,
they want us
near them.
They don't
want to hear.
Sometimes
girls show
just too much
emotion, then
they hear wrong
and cause
commotion, but all we
want is peace
and devotion.
Are all girls
a waste of time
or will true
love come to find?
Bearing in mind
most girls are kind
except for the ones
with a dirty mind.

Jerome Bellot (13)
Northfields Upper School

WHO'S THERE?

Slowly but surely I crept along the path, further into the black
                                                                       inky darkness
Branches hanging overhead like the knobbly hands of an old man
I needed to find her; I wouldn't give up now
She'd run like a scared rabbit into the darkness
On and on we went, me trying desperately to find her
Branches snapping underfoot like the sound of a whip
Leaves lightly brushing across my face
Brambles catching on my trousers trying to pull me down like a
                                                                       gripping hand
In and out the trees she goes bounding along like a deer
She is still in my sight, a silent shadowy figure
My heart is pounding like a drum in my chest
I cannot breathe, it feels like a hand squeezing the air out of my lungs
Will I ever catch up with her?
All I can see is blackness all around, it's like a tunnel with no way out
I am shaking, shivering, sweating, waking from my nightmare not
                                    knowing who she was or what happened to her.

Megan Scrivener (13)
Northfields Upper School

MY MUM

My mum is my best friend
She has curly brown hair
If I ever have a problem
I know she'll always be there

My mum has hazel eyes
That sparkle in the light
I know she'll always be there for me
Whether it be day or night

My mum will tell me off
If I don't get my homework done
But I'll never stop loving her
Because she's my mum.

Rachel Scheidegger (13)
Northfields Upper School

FAVOURITISM

(Poem based on a piece of art, Mary Cassatt's – The Family)

Brother . . . before you came alone,
I was Mummy's number one.
Now you're her little bundle of joy,
I always knew that she'd preferred a boy.
You always cry and whinge and wine,
Mum always hears your tears, she never hears mine.

I feel like a toy that's been used and grown old,
Put back in the box, left out in the cold.
Really I should hate you, but it's not you I should blame,
Does anyone in the house still remember my name?
Maybe I'm jealous, an emotion hard to admit,
You're the star of the show, so yeah I am a bit.

Is Mother not interested in the things that I do?
If the answer is yes, then I know it's because of you.
I feel like a failure . . . a nuisance . . . a pain,
All I want is my old life back again.

Brother, I hope you don't hate me, as such,
The most important thing is you were loved very much.

Sarah Steffens (15)
Northfields Upper School

TERASSE DE CAFÉ LE SOIR

In the dark of the night sits a café
Illuminated by candlelight, standing out from its blackened surroundings.
The hot, sticky air crept in with the darkness,
Settling thickly on the cobbled streets.
The warm breeze like a gentle hand,
Caressing the trees making them shiver with delight.

Gentle music drifting through the air,
The clip-clop of an approaching horse,
The soft mumbles of friendly chatter
And the warm aroma of fresh coffee.

A young couple sat, so in love
And stared into each other's eyes;
A reflection of the deep blue sky
Littered with flickering fairy lights,
A thousand candles in the wind.

Nicola Botcher (16)
Northfields Upper School

NOWHERE

My heart is empty and hollow,
I don't know where to go.
All is happy on this day,
I walk along the streets all day,
All I hear is laughter and joy,
It's Christmas Day and I have
Nowhere to stay.

Steven Baker (13)
Northfields Upper School

IF WINTER WAS A PERSON

If winter was a person I think he'd be a thief,
He'd snoop around, steal all the flowers and
Replace them with glittery snowflakes.
He'd strip the trees bare so they shiver
In the cold, frosty wind
And steal away the sun so that it will
Be freezing all day long.
If winter was a person I think he'd be a thief,
He'd take little children's Christmas presents,
So they would cry themselves to sleep.
Winter would make rain in the day and freeze it overnight,
So the roads become slippery traps for speeding cars.
If winter was a person I think he'd be a thief.

Stuart Jones (13)
Northfields Upper School

THE STAR DANCER ON THE STAGE

The twirling, swirling, whirling motions,
As she slides and glides from side to side
Then a leap and a flick,
A slow graceful kick,
The elegant dancer alone on the stage.
The audience stare and glare,
All eyes are on her,
As they silently watch and murmur in awe,
All those years of hard training,
Whines and complaining,
Now worthwhile,
For this moment she'll treasure, ever more.

Lian Wollington (16)
Northfields Upper School

M25

Beeppp . . .
Blooming traffic!
What are you . . .
Blind
Indicate ya old . . .
Move ya rear end!
Get outta my lane
Are we nearly there yet?

Beeppp . . .
Blooming traffic,
Well nobody's perfect,
What are you?
Mum. Where's my shoe?
Blind.
Indicate ya old . . .
Close the window I'm cold . . .
Get outta my lane
This is such a pain,
Are we nearly there yet?

One more junction to go,
Oh I've missed my turning,
Men, think they own the roads,
Bossing around like toads.

One more junction to go,
Oh nooo!
I've missed my turning,
The engine's burning,
Men, they think they own the roads,
Move out the way, I'm driving a lorry,
Carrying heavy loads
Bossing around like toads!

Victoria Dale (13)
Northfields Upper School

LOFTUS ROAD

I walk up to the stadium
hoping that we'll win.
I buy my programme and my ticket
and walk through the twisting turnstiles.

I walk up into the upper loft,
via the burger van and get a sizzling burger and my Coke.
Then I walk to view my pitch,
where Jude the cat is entertaining and shaking hands with little kids.

The stadium fills as the players warm up,
they go back in the changing rooms
and run back on the pitch.

The fans cheer and salute the players,
as they prepare to give their all.
To put the hoops back on top of the table
and please the Rangers faithful.

At the stroke of half-time the ball goes in,
Thommo with the goal.
The fans sound an almighty roar,
as the ball flies in the net.

The whistle blows for half-time
and the players leave the pitch.
The second half stays the same,
Queen's Park Rangers with the win.

Tom King (13)
Northfields Upper School

GARKE HUBBLE

I drew my clawd
To fight the garke
Monday noon it is
I met the garke
Which twoodes and ers
Down my spine, a shingle went
I am really beard
One, two, one, two
Closer, closer
Oh no, it's here
No clawd to help
Panic with fright
Beating pump I spit
Again be sure
Garke dead
Resting on floor
Sickle I feel
Charmp I am
Proud and gloried
At last
Garke killed
Finishly.

Lisa Holland (14)
Northfields Upper School

OOEY GOOEY

Ooey Gooey was a worm,
A mighty worm was he.
He stepped up on a railway track,
A train he did not see.
Ooey Gooey!

Peter Byrne (13)
Northfields Upper School

THE FOOTBALL MATCH

As the ball came
up to him, he did not
hesitate.
He stood up straight,
he passed the ball
to and fro waiting
for the day
he would score
a goal.
As the ball was
passed again, he hit it in
the top of the net.
The crowd screamed,
the keeper went mean
and shouted at all
of the team.

Karl Nielsen (13)
Northfields Upper School

THE BASKETBALL PLAYER

As he shoots his shoe comes undone
Then he smiles just for fun
He feels hungry and wants an iced bun
As he runs off the court he trips and falls
And hits his head on many walls
Then he runs back to the court
No he didn't abort
Come on, he's only short
He shoots, he scores
The whole crowd roars.

Michael Smith (13)
Northfields Upper School

LOVE IS...

A warm feeling inside,
A big box of chocolates,
A dozen red roses,
A candlelit dinner watching the sunset,
A bird's sweet song,
A smile in the morning,
A perfect match,
The most precious thing on this Earth,
A sweet fragrance,
An early dawn,
A child's birth,
A butterfly in your stomach,
Love
   Is
      Wonderful.

Kirsty Denning (14)
Northfields Upper School

WINTER IS A POLICEMAN

Winter is a policeman,
Icy and cold,
Handcuffing all the flowers
And throwing away the keys.
Locked up the sun
And chased away the cheerful kids.

Katy-Anne Jennings (13)
Northfields Upper School

THE CHASE

Running down the high street
Dodging people in the way
Sprinting
Climbing
Tripping
Tired
Can't go on anymore
Scared
Going to die
Help
I can't take the pain
I'm going to collapse
Falling
Falling
Fell.

Chris Taylor (13)
Northfields Upper School

PREJUDICE

P is for prejudice in the schools
R is for racism which isn't cool
E is for everyone that's felt the pain
J is for jealousy which is to blame
U is for under-achievers, can't do it right
D is for the drugs that make you fight
I is for intelligence that is wasted
C is for the children that have had to face it
E is even now we can't stop prejudice.

Chris Butcher (13)
Northfields Upper School

Faster, Faster

We get in,
Strap comes over,
Here we go.
Up, up, up,
We're at the top.
Oh my god,
Look at that drop.
Chain comes loose,
Aaahhh!
People scream.
My belly's coming up
Out my mouth.
So, so fast,
I can feel the G-force
Pulling my cheeks back.
Yuck, someone has just thrown up.
We reach the bottom,
Jerk to the side,
Ow! Hit my head.
'Ready to go round again'
Says a voice.
I'm going to be sick.
Upside down,
Whirl around,
This is great,
Definitely coming on again.
Yeehhaa,
Round the corner,
Brakes jerk on,
Get out,
Legs feel like jelly!

Nicola Brady (13)
Northfields Upper School

WE'RE OFF

Clucker de cluck
Clucker de cluck
over the edge
we're o
      f
        f.
Up
and
down
screaming and shouting
oh excuse my French!
Here comes the dipper
uhh, I want to get o
            f
              f.
Another kid crying
my heart was pumping,
here comes the black hole,
swerving,
dodging,
shivering,
speechless for words,
oh someone give me a bowl.

We're coming to the end,
I think I can hear the
brakes squeaking,
hang on a minute
I can see the world.

Let me off, I'm going to be sick!

Victoria Winchester (11)
Northfields Upper School

LOVE

I'm madly in love, I'm waiting for an applaud,
For her name is special, it is E Ford.
Our love will be forever,
You are my little treasure.

Words and letters cannot describe my love,
For we will be together until we're above.
She has lovely hair of black and brown,
She's so lovely, I could worship the ground.
Her fair legs tread on,
With her lovely voice of song.

I would like to take her away,
So forever we could love and play.
Living in the land of happiness and romance,
As she loves me by chance.

Sean Barton
Northfields Upper School

MY WINTER POEM

Winter is a fireman
Spraying and burning the sun down
Shutting the sun out for people's pleasure
Driving away the sun with his fire engine
Spraying snow all over autumn's leaves
And taking away summer's glory
Then when he has finished tormenting the children
He starts ruining the old people's sunlight
The fireman is a cruel, self-hearted man
He makes sun a thing of the past
And winter starts taking over.

Sean Bishop (13)
Northfields Upper School

My Best Friend!
(Dedicated to Lynsey Alexander)

My best friend,
I'd like to lend my life to her,
I can't bear to see her suffer.
She's been through so much.
Her dad's forgotten,
Her step-mum's rotten,
But then her little sister!
She's trying to get through it,
But my mate she knows it.
Her mum is watching,
From up there in Heaven.
My mate knows life does go on
And so does her love for her mum.

Channan Harkin (14)
Northfields Upper School

The Beast

He raised a hand which was just a claw,
The others ran towards the door.
He had mutated into a beast,
Looking for a human feast.
He roared and howled in a murderous rage,
Like a wild animal trapped in a cage.
He chased the others into the wood,
Although they knew it would do them no good.
One tripped and hit the floor with a thud,
The beast pounced and all that was left was a drip of blood.

Carl Denning (13)
Northfields Upper School

THE MURDERER

One night
When there was no light
The floorboards creaked
As the murderer sneaked
The door slammed shut
His finger got cut
He went back home
And made a big long moan

He comes back again
To cause some pain
The floorboards creaked
As the same man sneaked
The door slammed shut
Oh, what a mutt
No one's in
He tripped over the bin
He crawls about
But he can't get out
The door is stuck
That's just his luck!

Emma Ford (13)
Northfields Upper School

BLACK

Black is the colour of a vampire bat,
It's also the colour of their home.
Black is the colour of a witch's cat,
Around the streets they roam.

Black is the colour of Dennis' hair,
It's also the colour of Gnasher.
Black is the colour of a newly-born bear,
Don't get too close or they'll bash yer!

Black is the colour of a creepy room,
The colour of death when we cry,
It's the colour of a witch on her broom,
It's the colour of our midnight sky.

Rachel Chambers (13)
Northfields Upper School

FOR SIGMAR!

'Twas on a blistering plane,
The two great forces met;
The Dwarves of 'Karah-za-Karhack'
The Men of Altdorf.

Charged they did and with a great
Smash! they clashed,
Long the battle raged on the plain of asteroth,
Great Mages blasting powerful spells at each army,

The mighty Dwarf Hammerers took on
The noble Riesguard Knights
What a fight!

Volley after volley left the chambers of
Altdorian multicannons,
Shell after shell was fired from the great
Dwarf mortars.

The din of war, the finish is near,
Suddenly, silence
Nothing but the battered standard of Altdorf standing
Torn
Ripped
But standing.

Callum Hayden (13)
Northfields Upper School

THE CHASE!

I'm running
running from the story
my uncle told me
about things
reaching for you
running faster
houses blurring by
tripping over the grass
reaching for me
faster
from the trees
grabbing me
with branches
like claws
running out of breath
trapped
in a cobweb
thorns
ripping my flesh
home
yes home
home sweet home.

Shameem Hassan (14)
Northfields Upper School

A VEIL OF DARKNESS

Lay a black blanket across the sky,
Sun, moon and stars all pass me by,
A veil of darkness is all I see,
The slow sway of the trees comforts me.

As I feel the sky pulling me,
With its tearing claws endlessly,
With all my might, I try to hold on,
But all at once, my life is gone.

Lisa Thomas (15)
Northfields Upper School

FIRE

I start at night,
When no one's around,
While they're asleep,
I leap on the ground.

I run to the undergrowth
And I breed,
And then my power spreads to the trees,
Before anyone knows, I've grown big.

People run around
And beg on their knees,
But I don't relent
And burn more leaves.

Animals run
And I reach out my hand,
With a flash there's nothing left,
Apart from the ashes of death.

Then as soon as I've started,
I've gone like a flash
And that's the end of my tale
Of a manmade disaster.

Paul Henman (14)
Northfields Upper School

I Saw a Dolphin...

I saw a dolphin,
Jumping and swimming,
A whole family,
Having fun,
Jumping, swimming, looking happy,
Splashing, talking all day long,
A playground with no school,
Nothing to worry about,
No work, just play,
Something new every day.

I wonder what they are talking about,
Maybe it's boys,
You'll never know,
What about toys?

I'm on a boat,
Look, there's one,
It's waving to me
And saying hello,
It's now or never Nellie,
Give me the camera,
I wanna look,
Let me look!

Now it's time to go,
His mother is calling,
Look, now he has gone,
Gone back home,
As the boat pushed the water,
I kept looking,
Not finding a thing . . .
Now we are home,
I'm going to tell my mummy,

Mummy . . . *Mummy*
We saw a dolphin today,
It spoke to me,
It said hello,
It did Mummy, it did,
I saw a dolphin today . . .
It spoke to me.

Elaine Lunt (13)
Northfields Upper School

CROWD VS THE PLAYERS

Minutes to go before the start of the match,
Atmosphere building up like water in a bursting pipe,
Members of the crowd shouting abuse towards the players,
Chanting like bees as the players walk onto the pitch,
Beckham and Hypia go head to head,
Charging at the goal,
Beckham crosses the ball, it soars through the sky like a bird,
Like an octopus catching a fish,
The net catches the ball,
Silence in the Liverpool crowd,
Sighs of relief from the Man United crowd.

10 minutes to go, still 1-0 to Man United,
Steven Gerrard running down wing,
Gerrard floats the ball in for Robbie Fowler's head,
Fowler jumps in the air like a kangaroo,
Gets his head to it,
Goal!
30 seconds to go,
The referee looks at his watch for the last time
And blows the final whistle.

Mark Moore (13)
Northfields Upper School

WHAT IF I MISS?

As I jump to and fro
Look at me go
As I bounce up and down
Nearly falling to the ground
I have to do a flip
What if I miss
And something I hit?
As I get higher and higher
1, 2, 3
Put up my hands
And throw over my hips
Now I have to land
On my feet
What if I miss
And land on my head?
I'll most probably be dead
As I go round and round
My feet touch the ground
Everyone gets up and claps
I jump up and down
With joy.

Kayleigh Smithson (13)
Northfields Upper School

AUTUMN

A ll the leaves turning brown
U and your mates starting to frown
T o the trees you and your mates go
U pick up some sticks and start to throw
M ates of yours hit the conkers
N ot me though, so I'm going bonkers!

Luke Gaffer (13)
Northfields Upper School

FIRE

Red, red fire, burning bright,
Like a glow-worm in the night.
Creeps through the bark,
Eating its way in the dark.
Sweeping through the forest,
Destruction is left behind.

Red, red fire, burning bright,
Speaks the devastating fright.
Crackles like a smoker's throat,
Chances of natural life are remote.
Sweeping through the forest,
Destruction is left behind.

Red, red fire, burning bright,
Killing the innocent out of spite.
Consuming the sticks and burning the leaves,
Habitats are lost and the stick insect grieves,
Sweeping through the forest,
Destruction is left behind.

Jenny Hopla (14)
Northfields Upper School

BLUE

Blue is the colour of the sky and the sea,
Colliding together like sometimes we see.
Blue is bluebells in a baby boy's room
And the tears running down his face like
The stream nearby his place.
Blue is the sadness of the soul singers,
When it's ice cold and their fingers go numb.

Liam Breckon (13)
Northfields Upper School

Pink

The colour pink is like
a rainbow in the sky,
like crystal drops.

Pink is the colour of candyfloss
melting in the mouth.

Pink is also like the
heart beating in the chest,
boom, boom, boom, boom!

Pink is like the love you
find one day. Yippee!

Pink is like bubbles
floating in the air.

Pink are the fluffy slippers
you wear on your feet,
nice and warm.

Katherine Mullender (13)
Northfields Upper School

Fishing

It's 5am and all is still
I grab my sandwiches and my reel
I'm in my car heading for the lake
There's no one around, so I won't be late
I find my swim and I get set up
I cast my rod and wait on my tod
The water's calm and the sky is blue
A tiny fish just won't do.

Gary Lawrence (14)
Northfields Upper School

THE STORM

Strong waves out on the ocean,
Seem to be brewing a magic potion,
The wind swims through the ocean,
Pushing the water in a circular motion,
As the water rushes round in a circle
And the sky is different shades of purple,
A bolt comes down through the night,
A sudden burst of strong bright light,
It cracks open the ground on impact,
Pulling the world apart.

Next comes the rumble of the hungry sky,
Trying to be heard, wondering why,
Boats are wrecked out at sea,
Tossed about, the size of a flea,
After a while the sea calms down,
The waves that were once high, now touch the ground,
All around everywhere is calm again,
And nobody quite knows when,
The storm will strike again.

Emily Wilkinson (14)
Northfields Upper School

SCHOOL

Everyone knows that school is boring
Usually we end up snoring
The teachers are crazy
When they call us lazy
I'm glad when the home bell rings
So I can go home and do other things!

Jennifer Webb (13)
Northfields Upper School

My World

When all angels die
And all the demons break free,
When God retreats his world,
Suicide is how we flee.

Nothing really matters,
No one really cares,
No matter where you go,
They're all laying hatred snares.

This world isn't right,
Where people cuss the dirt,
One more case of bad over good,
One more case of hurt.

The worlds are at war,
Again, the sound of death rings,
Will the hatred end
Or will Satan still reign as king?

If God is really real,
Then where is he when we need him?
The question gnaws my thoughts,
As the light fades to dim.

My world now has changed,
I may not be here next year,
Politicians rule the world,
While my world waits in fear.

Sarah Hadland (13)
Northfields Upper School

I WISH

Could there be peace?
When would it be?
Today, tomorrow or the day after?

I wish we could see
And understand
What we are doing
To our native land.

I wish we could think
Of others
While thinking about
Ourselves.

I wish that there would
Be no more guns
And drugs that make
Our world aggressive.

I wish and I dream
About that very day
That all will be well
With this world, we called home.

But could that day
Be today, tomorrow
Or the day after?

Natasha Miles (15)
Northfields Upper School

NIGHTMARES

The noises are coming from the bush
Thank God it's the wind, with a great big whoosh
The moon is shining like a star
It looks so big, yet it's so far
Walking through the dirty crops
When will this adventure come to a stop?
There I am in the wood
When I came to a man wearing a hood
I ran through the river
Then I started to shiver
A branch hanging low over my head
It must have been a dream, I'm still in my bed.

Ashley Jenkinson (13)
Northfields Upper School

TOM AND TWITCH

I have a cat named Twitch
She always has an itch
She is black with patches of white
She sometimes gets into a fight
She always sits on my lap
If she gets angry, she will snap
I also have a cat called Tom
When he curls up, he looks like a big black bomb
He has big green eyes like apple pies and really soft paws
Sometimes he brings out his really sharp claws.

Kerry Lambert (13)
Northfields Upper School

BLUE!

Blue is the colour of tears running down your face,
The water dripping down the taps,
Blue is the hailstones patting down you back,
Like bee-stings all over and over again.
Blue is the coldness during wintertime,
It is also like ice cubes sitting in the fridge,
Blue is the seashore,
Which is salty, cold and long,
Blue is the sky on a lovely day
And blue is the swimming pools,
Where we all love to go!

Emily Waller (13)
Northfields Upper School

BLUE

Blue, blue is the sadness
in my heart.
The colour of crashing waves
on the shore.
Blue is the colour of the
tastiest mint I have ever had.
The colour of Heaven
and the sky
and the glittering sapphire
in my ring.

Michelle McGann (13)
Northfields Upper School

WHITE IS...

White is the snow on winter trees
White is the colour of the bones for you knees
White is the lightning flashes in the night sky
White is the moon in the sky so high
White is marshmallows all melted and squashy
White is sleet all watery and slushy
White is the mist on cold winter's days
Which makes everything a bit of a haze
White is paper fresh from the mill
White is the colour of a headache pill
White is our school shirts all crisp in the morning
White is the colour of marble flooring
White is new trainers just out of the box
And white is the tail on the end of a fox
White is a wave breaking on a sandy beach
White are the stars just out of reach
This is a poem by Nicholas Bunce
So I hope you don't think I'm a bit of a dunce.

Nicholas Bunce (13)
Northfields Upper School

BLUE

Blue is the colour of a cold winter's day.
It's the colour of big, tall waves crashing against the rocks.
It's the colour of a dark lightning sky.
It could even be the colour of your eye.
It's the colour of you when you are feeling ill.
Blue is the colour of a hot sunny sky.
It could be the colour of you when you die.

Daniel Ellis (13)
Northfields Upper School

THE NEVER-ENDING ROLE
(Postcard Poem Manet Un Bar aux folies-Bergère)

Evening Sir, what can I get you?
Same please Miss,
Same drink, same people, same bar,
The smoke-filled air chokes me every night,
The uncivilised conversations of the civilised make me sick,
The laughter of women rings through my ears,
Unwanted conversations with half-drunk men,
Every customer has their own story,
Like characters in a play acting out their parts,
When will this play end?
When will my character get to leave?
Soon I hope,
Evening Sir, what can I get you?
Same again please.

Caroline Impey (15)
Northfields Upper School

BLUE

Blue is the colour of rain on a winter's day,
The colour of the Scottish flag,
Blue is the colour of the clear sky,
The colour of seas and oceans on Earth,
Blue is the colour of ink we use in our pens
And singing the blues when you're feeling down,
Blue is the colour of sapphire on a ring,
Blue is cold,
Blue is happiness
And sadness on a sudden widow's face.

Matthew Burton (13)
Northfields Upper School

THE FAIR

An excited feeling inside of you,
when you hear a fair is due.
You wait and wait till the end of school,
you rush home and dress to look cool.

Blinded by the lights so bright,
people screaming from their fright.
All the rides, they seem so big,
going round and round above our heads.

People turning all shades of green,
like an old mouldy bean.
People laughing, having fun,
soon it's dark as in goes the sun.

Smell of candyfloss and smoke in the air,
everyone rushing, no time to spare.
On the ride, it goes so fast,
time to forget what's happened in the past.

Disappointed looks everywhere,
as down comes the funfair.

Levi Murray (13)
Northfields Upper School

FOOTBALL

I got to the gate
Said 'Alright mate, two tickets for me and him'
'Thirty-five pounds will be the charge'
As we walk towards the burger bar

People cheer while drinking beer
And trying to find their seats
We're over here you hear people say
And a fat man calls the linesman gay

In goes the ball, back of the net
People jump and shout
Van Nisterooy scores on his debut
That's a fifty million bonus for you

The final whistle blows in the pouring rain
Away fans boo and hiss
As everyone exits
1-0 the final score, we're back on top again.

Sam Taylorson (13)
Northfields Upper School

THE FIREWORK

I am a firework in a cardboard tube,
I can't wait to be set off to go zoom, zoom, zoom.

I was sent to a shop with many others,
We all looked alike, some were my brothers.

I was put on a shelf and then bought by a man,
He put me in a bag in the back of a van.

Then it was the night, I couldn't wait,
I was ready to go, I was all in a state.

I was all set up just about to be lit,
The people were crowding and fighting to sit.

A man came up to me and put a light to my tail,
I felt myself burn as I began to sail.

I rose into the sky and burst into stars,
Looked down at the people saying 'oohs' and 'aahs'.

Then I started to fall back towards the ground,
Then I faded without a sound.

Christine Baker (13)
Northfields Upper School

THE ALLIGATOR'S PREY

As the alligator watched its prey,
The tail of the lion began to sway,
The squeak of the mouse,
The buzz of the bee,
The elephant's trunk way up a tree,
The giraffe's long neck high in the sky,
As the grizzly bear makes honey pie,
The hiss of the snake,
The cheep from the bird,
Isn't this jungle quite absurd?
When the lion's tail stop swaying,
The mouse stops squeaking,
The bee stops buzzing,
The elephant's trunk comes down from the tree,
The giraffe's long neck comes to the ground,
The grizzly bear stops making pie,
The snake stops hissing,
The bird stops cheeping,
The jungle is quiet, all apart from . . .

Lauren E Burrows (13)
Northfields Upper School

PINK

Pink is the sparkle of an amethyst
Pink diamond is the sweet smell of roses in the summer
Pink reminds me of my favourite sweets
Pink is the smell of soft baby lotion rubbing on my skin
Pink is a baby colour, we were brought up with
Pink is a symbol of love.

Sophie Boddington (13)
Northfields Upper School

BLACK

Black is death;
It envelops you in its velvet touch.
Imagine a Dracula's cape,
Filled with the stench of death.
Black is your shadow,
It will never leave you.
Black is evil,
Filled with fear.
Living in black darkness,
Is impossible.
Black is *complete*.

Princy Gor (13)
Northfields Upper School

FEAR IS . . .

A shiver down your spine,
A butterfly in your stomach,
A dark alleyway,
Being the new kid at school,
A cold sweat,
A body full of goosebumps,
A haunted house,
A hairy spider,
A strange man,
Fear is scary!

Lydia Conlon (14)
Northfields Upper School

THE TIGER

I am a fierce tiger,
I once prowled through the wood.
I kept away from hunters
For my own good.

I chased the sweet rabbits,
I hunted every day.
But there's a side to me,
That stays locked away.

Just because I'm a tiger,
The fiercest predator here,
People naturally assume
That I feel no fear.

I have feelings too,
And a heart that goes 'boom'.
So why do they, when people see me,
Feel afraid and add to my gloom?

I'm not complaining, don't get me wrong;
I just don't like being alone.
I'm fed, given water, looked after quite well,
And if I'm good, they'll even give me a bone!

My only problem is this cramped cage,
Stuck every day in this little zoo.
I wonder what being free again would feel like,
But to be honest I don't have a clue.

But I'm a happy creature at heart,
I've got nothing much to moan about, of course.
I sleep and slouch and show off for visitors,
And then afterwards eat like a horse.

Please come over to my cage
Next time you visit the zoo,
Because if you come and watch me in awe,
I'll probably have happy memories of you.

Shelley Whitehead (13)
Northfields Upper School

I WENT TO FAIRYLAND TODAY!

I went to fairyland today,
Just to see the queen,
She was so beautiful, like the big open sea,
I was told it was a secret,
Under no conditions to tell,
I played and danced the entire day,
Afterwards they went,
Home that is.

They came today,
Just to perceive me,
There was a gigantic bang
And a wizard appeared,
He frightened me,
Then he said in a deafening voice,
'Can I play?'
I chuckled, it ought to have been a joke,
A wizard play in the company of me;
I went to fairyland today,
I must have fallen asleep,
As after I woke, they had disappeared.
I went to fairyland today!

Sarah Bithrey (13)
Northfields Upper School

BOUNCY BALLS

Bouncy balls are small and funny,
They bounce so high.
Sometimes they bounce as high as the sky,
They are sometimes blue, green or maybe rainbow,
Never play with them at the side of a road,
You might run out to catch it . . .
Bang! You might die from a car.
You have no idea it's coming . . .
Coming as fast as a rocket.
But you could play with bouncy balls anywhere else.
It can fly as high as the clouds,
It can sink to the bottom of the sea like a ship.
It can roll like a fat man,
It can race faster than a speeding bullet
Or it can be slow like a snail or a turtle.
Maybe one day bouncy balls will become a sport,
Like bouncy football or something like that.
But I know that bouncy balls are great,
And can be used for everything.
Those colourful bouncy balls.

Sam Girvan (13)
Northfields Upper School

CHRISTMAS TIME

Christmas is a time of joy
With all the lights you want to fly by at night
The snow tickling the cold ground
Father Christmas bringing streams of toys

The toys bang down the chimney
Angel being placed on the Christmas tree
The reindeers slide along the icy roofs
As Father Christmas sings merrily along

The turkey getting ready to be cooked
In a sunshine of heat
Children waiting to see who their visitor will be
The dark black sky as night falls by

The next day brings a flower of hope
Chocolates falling off the tree
The house swamping with happiness
Never-ending love.

Katie Huggins (13)
Northfields Upper School

A DAY OUT AT QPR

I turn up at Loftus Road,
to watch the Rangers play their game.
We walk to the club shop for a browse around,
thirty minutes till kick-off, we'd better get going.

We walk through the tangly, twisty turnstiles
to meet Jude, the fat cat who smells like a rat.
I smell the freshly-cut grass and listen
to the musicians with their brass.

The second half begins with
Andy Thompson here again.
We sing along with the crowd,
Come on you R's is the cheer
And the lady behind is shouting in my ear.

The final whistle is blown,
time for the winners to act like clowns.
Cheering and chanting down the street,
into a policeman at his feet.

Ryan Sheahan (13)
Northfields Upper School

A FRENCH CAFÉ

In a busy French café,
Where I stood and observed the scene,
I watched the French men dancing,
To fall in love so keen.

Some were watching the pretty young women,
As they swoop, swirl and glide,
But I felt my young heart pounding,
As one of them caught my eye.

He gave the slightest nod
And there was a smile beneath his lips,
His crystal blue eyes glittered,
As he put his hands upon my hips.

I gasped
And slapped him cruelly,
As he snatched his hands away,
But my delight must have shined through,
As together we began to sway.

We joined in the beautiful dancing,
In that busy French café,
Two months after we were married
And return there every day.

Fiona Broni (15)
Northfields Upper School

THE SEA WILL DECIDE

Fire and water, cracks and bangs
The fleet arrive in their many gangs
Screams and shouts, mist and smoke
The captain's crew slowly choke.

Harmless boys and savage men,
Find themselves in this war again.
'Arm the cannons! Fire your guns!'
The captain bellows his harsh commands.

The ships move like a snarling beast,
Festively fighting for its feast.
Will it ever end? Will it stop?
The war moves from dock to dock.

Unfortunately not to their delight,
The fight lasts from night to light.
As the war goes on and on,
The sea decides they're going home.

It pushes and pulls, the savage men
And stops this war from coming again.
In the end, all full of holes,
The ships fall to the seabed, along with many souls.

Amy Sewell (15)
Northfields Upper School

When Thoughts Die

As the day comes to an end
And life stands still
The light has disappeared
And the darkness invades the room

Music fills every corner
But they don't understand
What goes on in my world
The fear that's haunting me

Fear of future plans may seem
Distant and unreal
But when thoughts die I'm left alone
With only silence to comfort me

The rain is falling down now
From a watering-can in the sky
Now the sound of rain hitting my window
Is the only thing I can hear

Every day I'm torn apart
By things so far away
Reality pulls me out of the dream
Of a once perfect world

Only in silence can these thoughts
That were lost be regained
But things are not so simple now
And love's lost once again

This aching I feel can't last long.

Leana King (13)
Northfields Upper School

ALONE

I am alone,
No one
Not even a fly,
I'm frightened and shy;
My mum is always somewhere else, never says hello or bye,
Not interested in my life;
My dad was killed when I was two,
Goodness knows what for and by who,
I've been moved from school to school, not had time to
Meet different people;
I keep my head down and stand alone, waiting, waiting
For the bell to go;
The playground to me is like Hell,
People walk past, they all laugh and call me names;
I wear old, dirty clothes too small and damp,
People just love to call me a tramp.
Then one day someone said 'Hello, would you like to play?'
From that day forth I was never alone, in everyone's
Eyes I was known;
I have lots of friends to help me cope with my problems
And guess what? The playground doesn't feel like Hell
Anymore but more like Heaven.

Charlotte Davis (13)
Northfields Upper School

THE LONE WOLF

The lone wolf wanders through the night,
Howling at the moon,
The glowing sphere is his only friend,
As he stands by the lagoon.

Abandoned as a pup, he was,
When the fire came around,
It glared an evil glare at them,
And destroyed all that it found.

The family was trapped among the flames,
He was small enough to get away,
But when the fire had had its fun,
There was no one left to play.

The lone wolf lives in mystery,
No one knows his name,
So he's left to wander through the night,
Over and over again . . .

Gary Hudston (13)
Northfields Upper School

GREEN

Green is the grass that grows on the ground
And the moss that grows near the swamps
Green is nature, trees and plants
Green is grass, like emeralds and jade
Green is envy
Green is illness
Green is our planet that we're slowly destroying.

Kim Loczy (13)
Northfields Upper School

Love Is...

An invisible heart
One big happy daydream
A feeling as light as air
Like butterflies in your tummy
A summer's day
Picnics with a loved one
A big cuddly bear
A hug at the end of a day
A gooey feeling like jelly
Love is hearts and kisses
Love is just a word!

Samantha Candler (13)
Northfields Upper School

A Goal

F rancis Jeffers on the ball
O h he shoots
O h no, the keeper has missed the ball
T he shot has gone in
B ut it is only one-nil
A ll of the Arsenal crowd screaming in happiness
L eaping out of their seats
L ike they always do when Arsenal score.

Georgie Atkins (13)
Northfields Upper School

BLUE

Blue is the loud crashing of the waves,
Blue is sometimes what I feel,
Blue is the light colour of the sky,
Blue is what the swimming pool looks like,
Blue are all the bluebells in the forests,
Blue in the shade of aqua marine.

Jade Simper (13)
Northfields Upper School

WAR

There were bullets
Flying past like the wind!
People getting shot
People getting blown up

Mud, lots of mud
All runny in-between the dead bodies
Of all the brave soldiers
A man lying there with blood

Dripping out of his chest
Crying in pain

All of a sudden
There were about 20/30 planes
Flying across the sky
Dropping bombs and followed by a loud *explosion*

Then a whistle went
They all jumped over the sandbags
The tank went over the front-line
That was the end of the war.

Jack Janes
Stratton Upper School

THE SHOPPING CENTRE

Take one hundred grannies
two hundred teenagers
five hundred adults.
At exactly 9am push
through doors of shopping centre,
let them spread into various shops.
Leave to shop for three hours,
add a few visa cards,
leave to shop for a further three hours.
At exactly 6pm tip out of shopping centre
into various cars.
Tip into small terraced houses for a further hour.
Tip into bed and there you have it,
the perfect trip to a shopping centre.

Vicky Staines (13)
Stratton Upper School

TUMBLING CRASHES
(September 11th 2001 – the horrific crashes on the Twin Towers)

Mountains of rubble
With twisted metal,
Fountains of blood,
Bodies pulverised into oblivion,
Clouds of thick smoke,
Emotions are bad,
Rivers of tears,
Guns of protection,
Noise so loud.

Where will we start?

Colin McLeod (13)
Stratton Upper School

ARROMANCHES

Arromanches is a nice place now,
The sea is calm, like a wide gentle lake,
The grass is as green as emeralds,
But go a few metres under your feet
And you walk into a battlefield.
Guns blare like terrible sirens.
Bombs dropped, denting the ground,
Men fall, are trapped, with no means of escape.
The sea is grey, murky with distrust, hate and sorrow.
The ground is littered with men's dead bodies,
Another man falls and another.

Arromanches is a calm and peaceful place now,
It's hard to imagine it as a battlefield,
But the tell-tale signs of war are around you,
Like the dents in the ground from the bombs.
Think of them sometimes,
Take time to reflect
On the people who lost their lives.

Megan Williams (13)
Stratton Upper School

DISASTER DAY: SEPTEMBER 11TH 2001

What is in the mind of these people?
Why do they do it? What is it good for?
As the aeroplane flew into it like a knife into butter,
It exploded into a thousand pieces.

What is in the mind of these people?
Why do they do it? What is it good for?
The buildings collapsed and buckled like
Paper being burnt to cinders.

What is in the mind of these people?
Why do they do it? What is it good for?
The rubble looked like a pile of Lego, but bigger.
Survivors? I doubt it! Why did it happen?

Dean Kahl (13)
Stratton Upper School

THE NEW YORK TWIN TOWERS

The towers stood in New York City
Big, tall and very pretty
Until one day they were hit by planes
And both towers went up in flames

The fire was burning in a rage
The people inside were like animals in a cage
They had no way of getting out
All they could do was scream and shout

After a while the towers fell down
Causing devastation on the town
The people crawled from the rubble of the tower
Looking as if they were covered in flour

Hundreds of people were crying
As pieces of rubble went flying
The mess! The mess! What a disgrace!
There's rubble and debris all over the place!

How will we clean this mess off the floor?
It will take a year or maybe more!
It's going to take hundreds and hundreds of hours
To clean up what's left of the New York Twin Towers.

Sarah Buckland & Rachel Bennett (13)
Stratton Upper School

FLORIDA, SUNSHINE STATE

Epcot, Animal Kingdom
MGM, Magic Kingdom
Experience Disneyworld
Go see Shamu at Seaworld
Disney characters to see
Chip, Dale, Minnie and Goofy
Roller coasters to go on
Montu, Kumba and Python
Smell of food from the buffet
Milk, orange, tea and coffee
The sound of cars speeding past
On the freeway, going fast
Many shops sell Disney toys
For mums and dads, girls and boys
Long parades and great light shows
Everyone wants to go
Travel on a jumbo jet
Memories never to forget.

James Worboys (14)
Stratton Upper School

ONE DAY OUT: RECIPE

Get them out nice and early,
Cram 6 into a 5-seater car.
Travel for 4 hours until hot!
Take out and go to the ferry.

Wait until ready and set off.
When you arrive let them out,
Stir them around the streets,
As they beat their feet along the pavement.

When finished and drained of energy
And it's time to come home.
Reverse the process and come back,
Then leave to rest for 10 hours.

Josh Crisp-Hihn (13)
Stratton Upper School

SATURDAY SHOPPING RECIPE

Take 3 friends
Pack on train with others
Leave for 20 minutes
Then pour onto platform
Move them to shops

Separate and let them visit
New Look
Tammy
MK1
Claire's Accessories
Partners
Boots
Superdrug
Woolworths

Mix back together at coffee bar for lunch
Leave them to simmer for 3 more hours
Place back in train
Leave for 20 minutes
Place in front of TV
Add fish and chips
Leave to relax for 3 hours
Allow to cool at 9.30.

Francesca Wells (13)
Stratton Upper School

RECIPE

Take a couple of hundred people,
Put them in a swimsuit
And cram them on a beach,
Fry them for a couple of hours
And leave to cool in sea water for thirty minutes.
Take a bucket and spade
And add sand,
Let marinate for one hour,
Before cramming into a car.
Leave to relax in front of TV
For about two to three hours,
Before putting kids in bath.
After twenty to thirty minutes of kicking and screaming,
Put to bed!

Michaela Talman (13)
Stratton Upper School

A POEM FOR SCHOOL

Take hundreds of little children
And pour them into a school.
Stir the children and a few teachers
Around for ten minutes.
Leave to settle for two minutes
Before transferring into a classroom.
Scrape remaining children in and allow to cool.
When ready to start the lesson
Bring to the boil with the teacher
Who has boiled and is about to explode with stress.
Then leave again for a further 20 minutes
And then it's ready to eat!

Cheryl Barfoot (13)
Stratton Upper School

RECIPE FOR STRATTON SCHOOL!

Take one grumpy teenager and push into bathroom.
Allow to lightly simmer under shower and then squeeze into uniform.
Lightly pour into kitchen and allow time to devour toast.
Shove out front door, leaving enough time to walk to school.
At about 8:45am ram through doors of Stratton School.
Persuade to go into classroom and then leave to boil with one
grumpy teacher.
Wait for bell and then move into next classroom.
Repeat the previous two steps four more times
And then allow to return to original state.
Leave to cool in front of TV and then coax into room to do homework.

Zoe Atkins (13)
Stratton Upper School

THE TWIN TOWERS DISASTER

Twisted steel girders shaped like arches, point up to the deathly sky.
The field of ash on which they stand is disturbed,
By footprints of families, desperate to know the truth.
The sky is dark, a sea of grey swirling above like a murderous mist.
The hope to find life is gone, for the people innocently trapped.
Dark windows of houses beyond, evacuated to conserve more life.
People are quiet, thinking of lives that were lost, of people they knew.
They look up, grieving, for their heart is torn, to see . . .
Twisted steel girders shaped like arches, point up to the deathly
dark sky.

Anna Woodall (13)
Stratton Upper School

A Recipe For The Typical School

Take 1 or 2 thousand pupils and wake them
up at the crack of dawn, pack them and get
them ready for a torturous day and drag
them out to school.
Cram them all into a tiny classroom with a large
bad-tempered teacher with a monobrow
and force them to do boring work while
threatening them with detentions.
Give them a few hours of boredom then when
they look just about as uninterested as they
possibly could be, give them all a lunchtime detention.
Let them finally out of their lunchtime detention
to go and get something to eat.

Alice Nuth (13)
Stratton Upper School

A Girls' Shopping Trip Recipe

Take a handful of giggly teenage girls,
Squeeze them into one large shopping centre
With a sprinkling of money.
Add extra pocket money squeezed from parents
And add a large dollop of New Look.
Apply a small helping of friends' opinions
And leave in front of mirror for 30 minutes.
Stir in an enormous helping of clothes shops
And add a pinch of jewellery shops.
Leave to stand for at least three hours
Before scraping into McDonalds.
Mix in a big helping of Big Macs and fries
And pour into a car to go home.
Finally, leave to rest in their own beds.

Holly Johannesen (13)
Stratton Upper School

Rugby Match Recipe

Take thirty full grown men,
Add a few cauliflower ears.
Pour onto a muddy rugby pitch
And leave to intimidate opposition for ten minutes.
Place one elderly referee between captains.
Add one coin and flip.
Allow to settle for two seconds
And make decision.
Blow on the whistle and start play.
After forty painful minutes allow to stand
In smelly, grimy changing rooms.
Remove players form room and place on pitch
For a further forty minutes.
Take men off pitch and allow to marinate in
Sweaty juices for five minutes.
Place in coach and allow to boil until soft,
Serve with a cup of your finest tea.

Dominique Braybrooks (13)
Stratton Upper School

A Shadow Of The Bomb

A sense of bitterness sweeps across the town
Trees hang low like burnt old beggars
Twisted from clouds of dust
Bodies lie soulless
They are puppets in a play
America will never be the same
How could this devastation happen?

Kelly Chapman
Stratton Upper School

On The Battlefields

Dead soldiers lay on the floor like sardines,
Covered with a metre-thick blanket of mud,
Only a few survived,
The rest of them covered in blood.

Healthy men are now helpless,
They try to make their way,
Blind as bears they go,
But they cannot see where the dead men lay.

The smoke flies around like a sea of mist,
Plants everywhere fried like eggs,
Bodies scattered here and there
And an assortment of arms and legs.

People say that it's good to die for your country,
But as the bodies rot one by one,
I don't think it must
Have been much fun.

Julie Groves (13)
Stratton Upper School

Twin Towers

The twisted steel lay dead on the ground
Covered with mountains of dust
The fires blaze all around
The enemy has broken our trust

The emergency services buzz like bees
Trying to extinguish the fire
They lay the bodies under the trees
As the flames reach higher and higher

From the clouds of smoky dust
Emerge wounded friends
Angry people filled with distrust
Things will never be the same again.

Tracey Spavins (13)
Stratton Upper School

DAILY SCHOOL RECIPE

Pour 30 children in a cold area
Leave for at least 20 minutes
Pile in a tin can with at least 30 more
Chuck in a few bottles and polos
Transfer into slightly warmer area
Roll out all the children till they reach the door and pour inside
Separate mixture into small groups
And beat them into a classroom
Every hour allow some air and change area of baking
In a few hours allow the mixture to run in the dining hall
Add junk food, fizzy pop, chocolate and anything unhealthy
Pile back into a new classroom or old one
Allow 5 minutes to refresh
Change dressing into something light and place in cold area
Allow to run and slide around
If some mixture is hard throw a ball at it
Change dressing to normal
And pile onto tin can, add more bottles
Pour off
Change dressing
Allow some time for mixture to play
Allow to harden in cosy bed
Maybe served with black uniform.

Louise Baker (13)
Stratton Upper School

FOOTBALL SUNDAY RECIPE

Take 12 boys, get them up
Stir them in cars
Mix them to Old Trafford
Wrap them in kits and boots
By 3pm twist them to the pitch
Ping! There goes the whistle
A mixture of play
Get the away team a goal
All ready and done, 1-0
Win for away team
There they all go
Squashed is the bus
Home sweet home
Bed comes next.

Shaun Allen (13)
Stratton Upper School

THE YORKSHIRE MOORS

The sorrow morn of a winter's day
Life will come in spring's May
As the trees lose their leaves
As the clean, cold air will breeze
The smell of bonfires in the air
As the leaves float peacefully to the ground
As the breeze floats across the open moors
As sheep search for food among the frozen grass
The old tin mines abandoned, cold and grey
All alone on the Yorkshire moors.

Samuel Jenkins (13)
Stratton Upper School

London

I wander thro' each cheerful street,
Near where the town is bright
And laughter in every face I meet,
Places of joy, places of light.

In every heart of every man,
In every infant's laugh of joy,
In ever place the fun will start,
The little blighters play with their toys.

How the chimney sweepers clean themselves off,
Every candlelit church stands out,
The smile on their face will never rub off,
A lovely place without no doubt.

But most thro' midnight streets I hear,
How the youthful harlots cheer,
Blasts the laughter in everyone here,
People of London cheer, cheer, cheer!

Scott Gore (13)
Stratton Upper School

Tidal Wave Of Death

Twisted steel towering high on top of crumbled blocks,
People covered in sheets of dust,
Flames rising high like clouds,
People stumbling, running, screaming,
Trying to escape the coming wave,
Waves of dust towering over the people below.

Becky Sutton (13)
Stratton Upper School

No Sun, No Sand

Sun, sand
Sea all
Me, my mum and dad
Both looking rather sad
No sun, no sand
Oh, I am so mad

The beach is stony
The sky is black
Oh, I wish we could go back

All I can hear
Is the rain against
The windowpane
Oh, this holiday has driven me insane

A week has passed
Oh, it went so fast
At last I can go home
Oh, I am so glad to be no longer sad.

Natasha Jones (13)
Stratton Upper School

Cyprus Rap! Memories Of My Holiday

We're going to Cyprus, in the air,
Radio 1 is DJing there.
It's the one and only Trevor Nelson,
DJ Jo Luck and McNeat are there.
We're not there yet, more tunes to come,
The king of garage, it's Djez!

We're at the airport,
Our plane's come in.
We're half-way there,
Football on TV.
The plane lands and . . .
Germany 1, England 5!

Michael Gostling (13)
Stratton Upper School

School

School is good
School is bad
School is really, really sad

In the shadows
Lurk the teachers
Waiting to give you lines
I see large 'No Running' signs

At school you learn
At school you work
At school teachers lurk!
Why on earth are we on this Earth?

Don't do this
Don't do that
Don't even think about it!

School is good
School is bad
School is really, really sad.

Kayleigh Clement (13)
Stratton Upper School

SCHOOL RECIPE

Get a thousand pupils
Split into two groups
Squash some into school bus
Leave to settle
Sieve others through streets of Biggleswade

Once at school
Slowly pour into classroom
Leave teacher temperature to rise
During the class registration
Squeeze into separate lessons
Add work books and paper
Leave to simmer during the day

At break and lunch
Mix all pupils up
And bring together in school canteen
Boil until red in the face

At the end of each day
Add homework to pupils' planners
Divide back into two groups
To cool down on journey home.

Gemma Potter (13)
Stratton Upper School

TURKEY

Speedboats race along the sea
With dolphins following close
People surfing and people swimming
The horrible smell of sun cream

The sand is hot
People running into the sea to cool off
The sun is burning,
There is no breeze
There are lots of red people in the sea!

Jenny Austin (13)
Stratton Upper School

THE SPAGHETTI JUNCTION

Take 400 vehicles
Cram them in a saucepan
Fill the pan with 10 tons of petrol
Leave to simmer till vehicles begin to clear

Stir so to clear the stress
When vehicles have cleared
You should be left with
An oily substance

Add a bit of water and oil
Pour into a sieve but keep the liquid
The mushy oily substance will explode if you don't add 70 tons of steel
Heat the substance on a plate
Crumble an OXO cube on
And then you have a main course meal.

Dan Jackson (13)
Stratton Upper School

DAILY SCHOOL RECIPE

Slowly spoon 26 mates into
fresh school uniform.
Fold into Stratton School.
Bake in classroom at stress mark 6
for a lesson.
Sprinkle with homework.
Then raise the stress mark to 8.
Take out of Stratton School
and divide between 26 sofas.
Leave to dry in front of TV
for a few hours.
Add chips and burgers,
then grill with parents and homework.
Place into beds
then leave for 6 hours.

Karen Patman (13)
Stratton Upper School

SILENCE

Silence is something that gives us pleasure,
The place with calming sounds we treasure.
Sweet smells fill the room,
From burning candles in the gloom.
Everything standing still in time,
Ends with the sound of a chime.
We leave the streets full of pain,
To reflect on thoughts put on strain.
If everyone stopped and stared,
The secrets of happiness could be shared.

Vicky Pearson (13)
Stratton Upper School

STARRY SKY

The stars so bright but close to touch
In corners, ceilings and walls
Silvery, glittery, shining bright
Glowing, burning day or night

The deepest blue carpet low
Snuggle, sleep or lie
The lightest, brightest aqua blue
For the morning high sky
Sense the aroma all around
Of flowers, trees, all nature
Senses, smells to relax and soothe

Lights flashing round and round
Orange, green, red and blue
Feelings, emotions in my head
Music strumming quiet but strong
Pop. R'N'B, rap and rock
But then there's none

I just sit or lie
Watching the time trickle by
This is my favourite place
Where I can be alone
Be me and relax
In peacefulness and tranquillity
And quiet while I lie
Unaware of the trouble around.

Natalie Giddings (13)
Stratton Upper School

SCHOOL RECIPE

Take 1000 school children
And squeeze them into school.
Divide them into 10 and
Trickle them into classrooms.
Allow 10 minutes to cool and settle down
Then transfer to the main hall.
Mix 2 years together and cover them in complaints.
Next pour them out into different lessons.
Sit each classroom ingredient next to another
Wait for the timer to go, ding
Then scrape them off and spread evenly in the dining hall
Clear up the mess then chuck them into the playground
Wait for the timer to go once more
Then bake in classrooms until fully cooked
Take them out to ice the pavements and fill the buses with the leftovers.

Claire Rowley (13)
Stratton Upper School

LYME REGIS

The boats bobbing along in the rough sea,
The breeze wind blowing the sand
And a man getting chased by a bee,
People watching the woodwind band.

Children climbing the rocks,
Sandcastles to be washed away,
Fishermen coming into the docks,
People say not very good weather in May.

Ice cream vans at the beach,
Boats going steady,
Older people sitting on the seats,
Lifeguards at the ready!

Laura Stackhouse (13)
Stratton Upper School

MOUNTAINS

In the mountains it's snowing and cold,
The trees are covered in raindrops,
You can hear the wind whistling,
The raindrops hitting the ground.

You can see the white mountains,
You can smell the dead, frozen animals,
When you touch the bumpy trees,
You can feel it freezing.

When you are so hungry,
You try and look for food,
But when you taste the berries,
You can only taste the crunchy frozenness.

Then you hear the wolves howling,
You know they're looking for food,
They're just as hungry as you.

David Buss (13)
Stratton Upper School

MY FAVE PLACE!

I recognise the scent anywhere,
That's where I wanna be,
My bed is my fave spot
And I can't live without my TV.

The colour on my walls is green
And that's the colour of my mum's face
When she sees the mess
Of my fave place.

When I go in my bedroom
Everything is still,
But then my puppy runs up the stairs,
Like me he needs to chill!

Amie Jeeves (13)
Stratton Upper School

HENLOW DOG TRACK

T he dogs are running round and round,
H e's out on the track,
E lectric running through their bones,
  go dogs go, as fast as you can!

T he smell of fatty chips wafts around,
R ound and round dogs go.
A t the finish line is number 1,
C ome on number 5, run boy run!
K ids are running and screaming at the Henlow dog track.

Richard Hill (13)
Stratton Upper School

MAJORCA

M ayhem at the ice cream store
A ll the clean, fresh, summer air
J olly people splashing in the clear blue sea
O h what fun, to stand and stare
R un for joy, the sweet shop's open
C hildren run on the sand,
A dults calling for their children to come back.

Rebecca Setchell (13)
Stratton Upper School

LOVE

The sweetest ever romance,
Or a heart with angels' wings?
A passionate affair,
Or a marriage sealed with rings?

That secret loving smile,
Or walking hand in hand?
Kissing in a starlit world,
Or playing in the sand?

Together in a busy crowd,
Or talking on your own?
Whispering simple words of love,
Or just knowing you're never alone?

Clean and simple, true and honest,
Pure and white, just like a dove.
So when pain is all you see,
Remember
The greatest thing is *love!*

Katherine Bosworth (14)
Vandyke Upper School

MOONLIGHT DREAMS - WAITING FOR DAY

Sitting in bed, reading by the moonlight,
I'm all alone, waiting in the night.
With the rustling of the leaves
And a light, almost hesitant breeze,
I feel afraid, terror of the night,
The time when I am without light.

Waiting for the morning light to shine,
When, once again, light will be mine.
I will still wait
And I can hear the people outside arguing because their kids are late.
I am still waiting for the sun to shine,
For the daylight to be mine.

I hear the rattling of the branches stretching out for my window,
I will hide under my bed and crouch down low,
So low I cannot see them anymore,
But the light is still shining through the open door.
Waiting for morning,
While the world is still dawning,
I am asleep,
There is not a peep.
Silence rules.

Victoria Miljevic (15)
Vandyke Upper School